Pervasive Leadership
Releasing the Power Within

PERVASIVE LEADERSHIP RECOGNIZES THAT EACH OF US CAN BE A LEADER INDEPENDENT OF OUR TITLE OR POSITION. EACH OF US HAS A KEY ROLE IN CREATING THE FUTURE.

Copyright © 2024 Three-Seven Research, Inc.

First Edition: November 2014

Originally published as: *"Unleashing the Power of Pervasive Leadership"*

Second Edition: September 2024

ISBN: 9798340036513

The cover depicts the Space Shuttle's power being unleashed to accomplish an important purpose. While the actual Space shuttle may be obsolete, the reasons for its success are timeless. This book, Pervasive Leadership, will help you and your organization achieve success by applying timeless leadership principles.

We are thankful for Amazon providing this picture of focused power being released for a worthy purpose.

Three-Seven Research, Inc. Publishing
www.threesevenresearch.com
1 Sea Marsh Rd
Amelia Island Fl, 32034

Other Three-Seven Research Publishing books available at *Amazon.com*

"Career Aspirations – Finding True Success in Your Career" by Bryce Shriver ©2021

"Spirit Forged – 40 Days of Spiritual Renewal" by Helton, Hughes, Shriver and Weaver ©2022

PERVASIVE LEADERSHIP
RELEASING THE POWER WITHIN

CONTENTS

Contents 3
Preface 5
Why Another Leadership Book? 7
What Leaders Do 11
A Leadership Crisis 21
Clarity of Purpose 29
Intuitive, Effective Processes 41
Exceptional Teamwork 55
Commitment to Organizational Success 71
Innovation and Renewal 85
Engaging, Encouraging Culture 99
Pervasive Leadership 117
Closing – or is it the Beginning? 131
Three-Seven Research 143

PREFACE

We live in challenging times! Exceptional leadership is essential if our organization is to succeed.

Yes, we live in an incredibly challenging time.

COVID continues to impact our lives – from our personal health, school for our children and our careers. In addition, there is high inflation, social unrest and political turmoil.

Supply chain issues and inflation inhibit the normal flow of our products or services. Ideological and political divisions tend to discourage the open dialogue needed to understand and resolve underlying issues.

These challenges are filtering down into our organizations. Employee turnover is high while many critical positions remain unfilled creating stress for those who remain. The threat of a recession creates added anxiety.

Perhaps you are seeing the impacts in your organization. Does your organization rally around a common cause? Is there clarity in how to move forward with clear and timely decisions? Is there a strong sense of teamwork and an energizing culture?

How can we survive, let alone thrive in these trying times? Engaged, effective leadership is the answer. No, not a dictator or micro-manager, but leaders throughout the organization who have clarity of purpose with the technical and interpersonal skills needed to encourage others to work together to achieve success.

That is the purpose of this book – to develop leaders throughout the organization – **pervasive leadership** – to overcome these challenges. It encourages collaboration to solve our most difficult challenges and seize the many new opportunities created by the current environment.

No matter your current role – an individual who performs "real work" to the highest-level executive - this book will inspire you to strengthen your leadership role and provide the energy to achieve your organization's goals.

You will learn how to clarify the organization's purpose, streamline its processes, motivate others and build a culture of respect and innovation.

Originally published as "*Unleashing the Power of Pervasive Leadership*", the concepts have stood the test of time. They have been applied and refined over the ensuing years. This edition includes significant new insights based on this recent experience.

You will enjoy this journey. Both you and your organization will benefit from the timeless principles provided within.

Bryce Shriver

September 2024

WHY ANOTHER LEADERSHIP BOOK?

The market is flooded with leadership books - literally hundreds of titles crying for your attention. Why, then, should you select this one? After all, it's shorter than most (perhaps that is actually a reason to read it) and not written by a celebrity. It does not promise instant wealth or easy success.

Yet, the concept is intriguing - **Pervasive Leadership**. What does this imply? Is it to be confused with persuasive leadership where we apply strong emotional approaches to entice others to follow? Does it imply that leadership should be communal with everyone free to determine the organization's direction, priorities and policies?

Or, instead, is it an empowering concept - one that frees our human spirit to excel by drawing upon our intrinsic desire to accomplish great things?

Pervasive (adjective): existing throughout something, e.g., Pervasive Leadership: leaders exist throughout the organization.

Indeed, it is the latter. *Pervasive Leadership* highlights the sweet spot in the leadership continuum where organizational leaders are skilled enough to develop a clear sense of direction and commitment throughout the organization. These leaders encourage collaboration and innovation to improve processes, products and services. They encourage those throughout the organization to take ownership for its success.

Pervasive Leadership recognizes that the role of a true leader is to clarify the organization's purpose, provide needed resources, establish a positive culture and gain the commitment of the entire team to accomplish meaningful goals. It recognizes that mature leaders relax control in the belief that those closest to the work will make great decisions when properly inspired and supported. Additionally, it is an essential step in developing a new generation of leaders.

A second reason for considering this short book is its relevant, performance-based approach. *Pervasive Leadership* is built around Three-Seven Research's hallmark **Seven Characteristics of Successful Organizations** (Summarized below). Combining these seven organizational principles with the magic of *pervasive leadership* encourages organizational renewal and sustainable success.

Third, these concepts are actionable. The *Seven Characteristics of Successful Organizations* and *pervasive leadership* concepts were developed over decades in the real world - conceived in failure, refined in success. The focus is on practical application, not esoteric theory. Each chapter includes exercises to assist in understanding and applying the principles - no matter what your title or position on an antiquated organizational chart.

Lastly, this book is designed for everyone who aspires to success, both as an individual and for their organization. Leaders, as defined by the organizational chart, will multiply their effectiveness. Perhaps these concepts are even more valuable for those buried in the organization – those closest to the actual work who long to make a greater contribution.

"Why a major update for this book? What has changed in the decade since this book was first published?", you may ask.

COVID and societal changes are one quick, accurate answer. Our work environment has dramatically changed. Many of us increasingly use internet-based technology to stay connected with our work and socially. There is less direct interaction. Thus, the concept of leadership being displayed throughout the organization is more difficult.

Secondly, we have continued to apply and refine these concepts in other settings. For example, in these days of social discord where compromise seems to be the only way to get things done, the concept of collaboration has become more important. We have increased our focus on the importance of **collaboration** and how it is best accomplished. This is one of the key areas where *pervasive leadership* is vital.

Another addition is the concept of **career aspirations** – those internal motivators that encourage each of us to give our best in accomplishing the organization's purpose. Our research has demonstrated the importance of understanding and applying these concepts in organizational, as well as personal success.

In summary, this book encourages you to apply today's best leadership concepts with time proven approaches to increase your personal and organizational success. Join us on this journey - it has the power to transform your life as it has ours!

This book is for you if you:

✓ Desire to be a more effective leader and recognize that encouraging leadership throughout your group will help achieve its goals in a more effective, enjoyable way.

✓ Do not yet have a leadership title but are looking for a stronger voice in the organization's success.

✓ Feel that your organization has lost its way with an unclear purpose, processes, culture or values.

Seven Characteristics of Successful Organizations

1. **Clarity of Purpose**
2. **Intuitive, Effective Processes**
3. **Exceptional Teamwork**
4. **Commitment to Organizational Success**
5. **Innovation and Renewal**
6. **Energizing, Encouraging Culture**
7. **Pervasive Leadership**

WHAT LEADERS DO

Clearly defining and fulfilling the leader's roles compels others to join their ranks.

It was a time of severe challenge in our organization – a power plant providing electricity to over two million customers. Safety, reliability and low cost were clearly established goals. We were meeting none of these.

We were not just failing as individuals, but failure had spread throughout the organization! If we were to retain our livelihood and our company, change was imperative.

But where should we start? Our product, electricity, was fundamental to society and our technology was proven in hundreds of locations throughout the world. Our organization had been successful in the past, being recognized as an industry leaders a mere decade before.

Yet, we were failing our customers, our company and ultimately, ourselves. Our costs were too high and our reliability too low. We would not survive unless both changed – either on our own accord or at the direction of a new owner!

In the end, the critical change leading to the organization's resurgence was the renewal of leadership. Not a new leader, but a change in our fundamental approach to leadership that energized the skilled workforce that had been successful a decade earlier.

First, we defined the leadership roles, not in terms of the organization chart, but in positive, forward-looking relationships. Only then were we able to identify and develop individuals to fill these roles. The transformation, both in performance and job satisfaction, came when we realized that leadership was not limited to certain individuals by virtue of their position, but was most effective when broadly shared throughout the organization – when the concept of *pervasive leadership* was implemented.

This is the story of our journey – a journey conceived in chaos, tested in crisis and rewarded with success. It is the story of common people who, with courage, commitment and purpose, exchanged the dejection of failure for the elation of victory. Yet, the journey is never over, for true success is continually redefined, its standards raised and its rewards expanded.

Our journey started with the simple recognition of what true leaders actually do rather than defining them in terms of organizational charts, responsibility statements or budgets. The following aspirational statements define the key leadership roles:

Leaders develop intentional relationships

- ✓ Leaders recognize that their most basic role is to bring people together to accomplish goals that cannot be achieved by individuals alone.

- ✓ They value people, their perspectives and talents, always seeking to engage others in achieving organizational goals.

Leaders create the future

- ✓ Leaders define the organization's purpose - providing a clear, compelling vision that inspires our best effort.

- ✓ They bring the vision to life - compelling and empowering teams to make it a reality.

- ✓ They define success in meaningful, measurable terms.

- ✓ They set expectations - presenting a clear picture of both the goal, its value and the process for its achievement.

- ✓ They demonstrate initiative, not waiting for a crisis before acting.

- ✓ They motivate us, draw us together, encourage innovation and create an environment that compels action.

- ✓ They look to the future and adapt to assure that the organization remains viable as the culture and economy change.

Leaders actively develop a positive culture

- ✓ Leaders are trustworthy, having integrity and good judgement. They place value on people above purely financial success.

- ✓ They are optimistic and enthusiastic, focusing on objectives and solutions to challenges.

- ✓ They develop a collaborative culture, based on respect and trust, where each individual commits their unique and significant talents to achieve excellence.

- ✓ They encourage innovation by actively listening and being open to new ideas and approaches.

- ✓ They provide the needed resources, technology and training.

- ✓ They encourage people to perform those roles essential for success while forgoing busy work.

- ✓ They engage themselves and their team by looking ahead to anticipate future needs and resolving issues before they become a crisis.

- ✓ They set an example, remaining true to their core values of integrity, respect, openness and optimism.

- ✓ They are committed to the organization and they expect the same from their team.

- ✓ They resolve conflicts and address performance issues.

- ✓ They are present and active during crises.

Leaders deliver exceptional results

- ✓ Leaders are competent – they understand the business and its people. They understand what is important, particularly in motivating and encouraging the team that actually produces the product or service.

- ✓ They are committed and an active part of the team, sharing in its challenges and successes.

- ✓ They break down barriers and provide support to achieve the near-term goals needed to realize the long-term purpose.

- ✓ They are accountable, asking "Did we accomplish what we set out to do?"

- ✓ They develop the team by encouraging collaboration and inspiring commitment.

- ✓ They lead collaboration to seek solutions in times of crises.

Do you see yourself in these descriptions? Do you long to make a difference - to be part of a winning team? Dreaming big dreams is a start. Next is defining leaders by what they do instead of their title.

Yet, there is more. The next step is that of personal commitment - transitioning from abstract philosophy to specific actions. It requires a change from general "third person" statements to "first-person" commitments to your organization.

Here is one example of how these concepts were applied as we resolved to save our power plant – to achieve the highest industry performance standards. I made a personal commitment and encouraged individuals throughout the organization to join me.

As a Leader, I am personally committed to sustained excellence

I am passionate and personally committed to our success. I will invest myself in creating a culture where we grow and our team has the resources to accomplish goals previously viewed as impossible.

To achieve this, my principles – the commitments I make to myself and to those around me – include:

- Entrusting my heart to our vision and our people, because if I don't, then there is no reason for me to take a stand. I ask you to display this courage.

- Creating energy through a positive, forward-looking attitude and a shared understanding of the importance of achieving our vision.

- Establishing challenging goals with clear expectations that require your action and support to get the required results.

- Building relationships that encourage collaboration and innovation. An environment that trusts individual talents, respects differences, develops skills and nurtures teamwork so that you will take initiative and empower our team.

- Recognizing that individual empowerment requires personal responsibility for achieving the organization's goals while meeting high standards of integrity. The freedom associated with empowerment leads us to higher performance standards.

- Committing to excellence through innovation and continuous improvement. Embracing the fact that knowledge comes from celebrating successes and learning from failures. I understand and appreciate that *excellence* is a dynamic concept that never rests.

- Engaging myself and expecting the engagement of those around me. We can succeed only if everyone gives their best.

- Proving myself through my actions. I will cultivate you by letting you join in my successes and failures to encourage your leadership development.

- Believing that, together, we can change the world – making it a better place for all.

As you will see, our commitment worked! In less than a year our performance returned to acceptable levels and within two years were recognized as being among the best in our industry. It was a truly rewarding experience for all involved.

Will you join me in this quest for meaning and accomplishment? That is the purpose of this book! How are you going to change your world?

Application: What Leaders Do

With any successful endeavor, active involvement is required. Likewise, each step in our leadership journey requires our personal understanding, application and commitment leading to action and change!

We encourage you to actively pursue the insights provided in each chapter - the rewards are great! Each chapter includes a few suggested actions designed to achieve these goals.

There are many approaches to gaining value from these applications. For example, you may want to use a journal to personalize the applications and reflect on the insights you gain through their use. Update your journal as you gain experience and insight. In addition, you may want to join with another person in this journey – sharing personal insights, successes and challenges.

You will be encouraged as you apply the applications and see the changes in your leadership success.

Let's start by contemplating what effective leaders do:

1. Reflect on someone you admire, someone who "gets things done" while encouraging those who do the actual work. How

do they model the roles of leaders summarized in this chapter? Explore how their constructive relationships with others contributed to their success.

2. Seek to support someone in a leadership role by encouraging them for a week. Ask open-ended questions and then actively listen to their ideas and provide positive feedback <u>without</u> explaining how they could do better. Volunteer to assist them in realistic, practical ways and then follow through on your commitment.

3. Reflect on how the leaders reacted to your involvement. How does this experience shape your view of a leader's role?

"Give instruction to a wise man and he will be still wiser;
Teach a just man and he will increase in learning."
Proverbs 9:9 NKJV[i]

A LEADERSHIP CRISIS

*Our organization and our society
is crying out for true leaders!*

It was a bad day – a necessary but delayed acceptance that we were unsuccessful. Our failure was obvious to all, costing the company millions of dollars and losing the respect of our stakeholders.

> *"If it were a football game, we would have lost 52 to 10, however, it was not a game, it was our livelihood!"*

If it had been a football game, we would have lost 52 to 10. Instead of learning from defeat, we were busy justifying our failure. The offense was happy to have scored 10 – if only the defense had stopped the opponent's long passes. The defense accepted that their performance was not outstanding, but the offense should have scored and, if they would have not fumbled twice, we would have had a chance. We longed to return to a decade earlier when we were the undisputed champions – the ones others desired to emulate.

But it was not a football game. It was our livelihood. We were unreliable and too expensive. We were out of options – we had to either improve our performance or fall into bankruptcy with other great American icons like Sears, J.C. Penney, Toys-R-Us, Circuit City, Pontiac, Rite Aid, Red Lobster and a host of others.

What was our underlying problem? How could our well-known company have periods of glory followed by organization-threatening poor performance? The people doing the actual work had not changed– many had been with the company for twenty years or more. There were no major labor disputes, there was no new technology trying to put us out of business. Yes, the machinery was getting older and the regulations more complex, but those were not the fundamental problem.

Leadership? Could ineffective leadership be inhibiting our performance? We were like a football team without someone calling the plays, a team where each player did what they felt best without considering whether it was a run, pass or punt. In hindsight it was predictable that chaos would ensue.

We lacked true leadership. Each work group was struggling to achieve their self-defined goals. There was little coordination among groups, little consideration of what could go wrong and developing options for resolving problems instead of pushing them to another work group. Operations could always defer to poor maintenance who, in turn, could defer to inadequate engineering or planning since their job was to "fix" things, not design them or ensure that all needed parts were available. Respect and trust among work groups or their leaders were not to be found.

A change in leadership, at all levels, was needed to solve this – to get us back into the game. We started by looking at ourselves. We asked critical questions, individually and as a group, concerning what needed to change. We asked people throughout the organization whether we had the capability for success. We confirmed that the power plant was well designed and that others of the same vintage were performing exceptionally well. Did we understand our business? Did we have the required skills and tools?

In the end, it was not a matter of capability, but of commitment to common goals. The fundamental roles of leaders in establishing a common purpose, developing commitment and building trust were absent.

We started a journey together, drawing from our experience – from those times that we were successful. We learned from others in our industry. Later, we explored other industries where safety and sustained high performance were essential. We then collaborated to apply these insights in our organization.

Within a year our performance turned around – not in a slow, evolutionary way but a fast transformational change. Nearly all objective performance measures improved by tens of percentage points and our profitability tripled. More importantly, it became a fun place to work again. We celebrated successes together and, as a team, worked to resolve remaining challenges.

What changed? Leadership!

> *Pervasive Leadership: Exceptional performance came when many people throughout the organization chose to lead rather than be spectators or victims.*

No, it was not a new group of managers that came in to "fix" the workforce. There was not a new star quarterback or point guard that energized the team with heroic feats. There was no field marshal to rally the troops or great orator to tickle the ears with fine sounding theories.

It was basic leadership – clarifying goals and identifying what was needed to accomplish them. We developed a broader picture of each group's unique role and interrelationships needed to achieve those goals. At that point, our weaknesses became evident. Improvement came when leadership permeated the organization - reaching across departmental boundaries to identify the underlying issues and collaborating to resolve them.

The change came because many people throughout the organization chose to lead instead of remaining as spectators or victims. It was through leadership of those closest to the work, who saw the process's weaknesses, and in their supervisors who had the authority to make needed changes. These changes were encouraged by senior leaders who helped establish a culture of respect and provided the required financial resources.

Sustainable success came when leadership was expressed throughout the organization at all levels, in all groups. There was energy, purpose and commitment where apathy previously prevailed. Our processes became more efficient when we respected the uniqueness of individuals and eliminated a multitude of administrative barriers that previously prevailed.

As we continued to improve, we found success was linked to the robust application of *Seven Characteristics of Successful Organizations* summarized here:

Seven Characteristics of Successful Organizations[1]

---

[1] *Seven Characteristics of Successful Organizations* is based on research

1. **Clarity of Purpose** – a clear and compelling reason for existing with goals worthy of our best efforts.

2. **Intuitive, Effective Processes** – consistent, efficient methods for achieving our goals using technology to enhance personal connection and judgement.

3. **Exceptional Teamwork** – people applying their unique skills and positive attitudes working together.

4. **Commitment to Organizational Success** – individual and organizational ownership for achieving common goals.

5. **Innovation and Renewal** – a willingness to try new approaches and encourage fresh ideas by breaking down obsolete paradigms and organizational barriers.

6. **Energizing, Encouraging Culture** – optimistic, respectful, collaborative and performance oriented.

7. **Pervasive Leadership** – people throughout the organization collaborating to implement the first six attributes.

---

conducted by Three Seven Research, Inc. and is the topic of an upcoming book.

Our journey never ended. We continued to face challenges but with the new approach and collaborative culture we worked together to address them and achieved excellent, sustainable results.

The summary of leadership roles and commitment that opened this book was the start of our rebuilding – of our renewed commitment to success. At that point there was a need for hope, a light to give a sense of direction in a dark time. The thoughts developed in that summary were not complete, having not yet endured the crucible of experience, but they opened the dialogue. The many discussions that followed provided an alternative to our underlying leadership weaknesses. Together, we expressed hope, built commitment and encouraged the emergence of leaders throughout the organization who eagerly joined the battle.

Organizational challenges abound in this third decade of the 21st century. Covid, cultural differences, supply chain challenges and the generational transition are but a few of these challenges. Millennials now outnumber baby boomers in the workforce bringing different career ambitions and skills to address these challenges. New technologies have transformed the way we work together.

No doubt, you too, are on this journey. You are seeking a better, more fulfilling life. You strive to achieve more, to add value, to encourage others and, together, achieve goals that today may seem out of reach.

Your title is not important. It is not a matter of position or authority. Leadership is not defined by the organizational chart whether you serve in a company, a non-profit organization or a social club. Leadership is about seeing what can be – the value that can be created – and enlisting others to join you in making it a reality. It is a journey worth taking.

Our purpose is to help in your journey – to stimulate your ideas and commitment. We encourage you to join us by developing the concept of *pervasive leadership* and applying it in your leadership role. It is a journey that will reward you and your organization deeply.

Application: A Leadership Crisis

1. Reflect on a time when your team (work, family, sports team) was successful. Grade the importance of each of the *Seven Characteristics of Successful Organizations* in that success. How was each attribute exhibited?

2. Consider a current personal or work challenge you face in terms of the same characteristics. Where are the strengths? What areas are adversely affecting performance?

3. Define how you can reinforce one characteristic that is strong and how you can strengthen just one that is not. Who do you need to work with to accomplish your plan?

"My son, if you receive my words, and treasure my commands within you, so that you incline your ear to wisdom and apply your heart to understanding; Yes, if you cry out for

discernment and lift up your voice for understanding, if you seek her as silver and search for her as for hidden treasures, then you will understand the fear of the Lord, and find the knowledge of God."
Proverbs 2:1-5 NKJV

CLARITY OF PURPOSE

*Energizing our organization by
internalizing our reason for existing.*

"Every person, every organization has a purpose for being, that is not the question. Is it a worthy purpose - one that provides meaning and benefits society?

That is the question to be answered."

Every person has a purpose? Yes, we are each unique – no one else has your personality, skills, experiences and passions. Each of those contributes to your value by defining your role in this grand story of life. Indeed, the question is not whether we have a purpose, but whether it is meaningful and whether we are achieving it.

The same is true with organizations, whether it be a government department, a company, a university or a church. We organize to accomplish something of value – a goal that cannot be accomplished by an individual. Again, the challenge is to define your organization's purpose in a way that inspires energy and commitment– to provide meaning in what we do.

You may have heard the ancient story of how three stone masons working on the same building responded when asked what they were doing.

- The first said, "Putting in my time, just hoping to get paid".

- The second responded, "Laying these stones perfectly, building a wall my sons will be proud of".

- "I'm building a cathedral to encourage the worship of the living God", exclaimed the third. "It will be a magnificent center of worship for generations to come!"

What is your organization's purpose? What goods or services is your organization providing that are of true value? How is it meeting the needs of its members and society as a whole? Why is this organization worthy of the effort that you and others are expending on it? These are the questions we need to answer, unless "putting in my time" or "just hoping to get paid" is all we expect.

> *The challenge is to define your organization's purpose in a way that inspires energy and commitment to achieve that worthy goal.*

While most organizations have "purpose" or "mission" statements, often they are not effective. In many cases the words are too general to be compelling and do not appear to be related to our everyday tasks. As a result, mission statements often decorate the walls or annual reports but have little relevance to everyday activities.

Examples of these limited value statements include:

"Becoming a world class performer"

"Healing people by providing stellar medical care"

"Being the best in our industry – the cable provider of choice"

"Rewarding share owners with outstanding returns"

"What is the purpose of a mission statement?", you may ask.

Is it to help the employees or public feel good? Or is it targeted and aspirational to encourage employees to accept a true calling – one that benefits others and cannot be accomplished without an organized, committed team. The latter is the definition we will pursue.

Words alone do not define organizational purpose, but they are a start. An effective purpose statement is more than just a catchy phrase. It creates a picture of what we aspire to accomplish in terms of benefits, not just actions. It should reflect who we are and why our organization matters. An effective purpose statement should have the following attributes:

- ✓ Compelling - developing an emotional tie by expressing why our organization matters - the value it brings to society. It provides reasons for us to give our best to achieve the goals.

- ✓ Clear and concise – creating a picture of success for the team members and those they serve.

- ✓ Encourage a "line of sight" between the activities of individuals and subgroups in supporting the overall goal.

- ✓ Reflect the organization's core values and culture.

- ✓ Focus on achievement instead of philosophy.

The words are not of paramount importance – it is the integration of the purpose and values into the culture that makes the difference.

Yet, too often, we overlook the essential element of clarifying the reason for our organization's existence and, in doing so, miss a prerequisite for lasting success.

Here are a few examples that are better developed:

"Creating a delightful pizza experience while drawing family and friends together"

"Providing an affordable automobile that is a delight to drive while providing safe, reliable transportation"

"Providing hope for dysfunctional families by…."

"Assuring the safety and energy efficiency of buildings constructed in Springfield County"

"Sharing the joy of knowing Christ and the promise of eternal life"

Each of these is a start – a statement reflecting the unique purpose and value of the organization. In some cases, such as the pizza parlor, the simple statement may be adequate. Others, such as "Providing hope for dysfunctional families", will benefit from additional clarification by adding information about who, how and underlying values.

An essential leadership role is defining a purpose that is meaningful to each member of the team – one that inspires them to excel. Like the stone mason, a pizza delivery woman will likely have a different approach to her job if she sees that she has a significant role in creating a delightful family experience instead of just delivering a pizza, collecting the payment and hoping for a big tip.

These example purpose statements may be a fine start for a small organization, or even a mid-sized organization that is well focused. But what about a large organization with diverse products or services? Consider the industrial giant General Electric. How do you create a purpose statement that is meaningful for both home appliances and jet engines? John Deere's advanced agricultural equipment, heavy construction equipment and financial arms are more closely related but may also struggle to develop a single, compelling purpose statement.

The answer is to develop the purpose statement at the highest level at makes sense and then focus the organization on achieving it. For example, John Deere's financial unit may have little to do with the design or manufacturing of tractors but has a great deal to do with enabling customers to purchase those tractors since about 50% of the new equipment sold by dealers in 2021 was financed by the company[2].

Thus, their purpose statement should make that connection while reflecting their unique role.

We will not write a purpose statement for John Deere's financial unit[3], but it could include the following elements:

- The importance of John Deere's advanced agriculture equipment in meeting the world's need for food. The

---

[2] John Deere, Inc. 2021 Annual Report
[3] Based on the quality of John Deere, Inc. website and annual report, we expect that they have implemented this concept far better than this condensed summary reflects. Our example is only intended to convey the concept more clearly.

importance of their other divisions, e.g., turf, construction, should also be included.

- The essential role that financing plays in allowing customers to purchase or lease this essential equipment and how this creates value for both the customers and John Deere.

- The unique values and processes that make John Deere finance the preferred lender for customers. This may be linked to the Corporation's "Higher Purpose" and principles published on their website[4]

- Lastly, the unique roles of individual groups within the financial unit can be developed to give those groups a *line-of-sight* to the broader Financial unit and Corporate purpose.

While a written purpose statement is a start, it is when leaders throughout the organization routinely refer to it as a guiding principle and demonstrate it through their actions, that it becomes truly effective.

We applied these concepts in clarifying the purpose of our electrical generation station. Collaborating with a small group of leaders from throughout the organization, we developed the

---

[4] www.Deere.com/en/our-company/higher-purpose/

following purpose statement: *"Advance society by providing safe, reliable and affordable electrical power."*

The written statement is simple. When discussed with employees and the public it became compelling by expressing the value of reliable power in terms of life-saving medical technology, reliable public transportation, advances in communication and the benefits of home heating and air conditioning. By doing this, we were defining an important role since a critical differentiator between an advanced society and third-world poverty is the availability of reliable power.

The linkage between this important high-level goal and the actual work done by employees was emphasized in large and small group conversations. We consistently referred to our purpose during decisions concerning maintenance activities, equipment upgrades, personnel training, leadership development, etc.

The hierarchy of goals; namely, safety then reliability and lastly cost were emphasized throughout the plant and integrated into the decision-making process. We added the concepts of respect, collaboration and a positive culture.

In the end, the simple statement, *"Advance society by providing safe, reliable and affordable electrical power."* was accepted in the broader context outlined above through consistent communications and, more importantly, using it as the basis for making decisions.

The value of this clearly stated linkage was realized when operations personnel took a keen interest in understanding the condition of key equipment and craftsmen took initiative to fix that equipment instead of deferring to engineering to justify its acceptability. This initiative enhanced safety and reliability and, as a result, contributed to lowering our costs.

This example is just one of a multitude demonstrating *pervasive leadership*. We started by engaging leaders throughout the organization in refining the high-level mission so that it had direct meaning to each team. Our intent was to establish a clear *line-of-sight* between each group's activities and the overall purpose of the organization. Individuals in all parts of the organization began making better decisions since they understood the organizational goals and saw how their efforts supported achieving our purpose.

Another important purpose of a meaningful mission statement is the ability to measure progress toward achieving the goal.

Collaborating with the team, we developed meaningful performance measures that allowed us to evaluate our actual performance by comparing it to the industry standards of excellence. It was easy to measure power production, in terms of gigawatt hours. Reliability was defined in terms of unscheduled plant power reductions. Safety and costs were also easy to define. Each of these metrics were linked to individual organizations.

Other important goals, however, were not so easy to measure. For example, our team's trust in management, as demonstrated by the openness to employees raising concerns about safety or the resolution of conflicts in priorities, etc. was not clearly defined. In these cases, employee surveys were used to provide the needed insights. The intent was to provide meaningful, honest feedback on our performance with the intent of improvement.

Formative dialog was used to refine a clarify the goals throughout the power station to ensure that they were meaningful. As a result, the broader, station goals and performance measures were expanded to be meaningful for each workgroup. The intent of this process was to:

- ✓ Link each workgroup's purpose to the station goals.

- ✓ Clarify the unique and significant roles the workgroup provided in meeting the station goals.

- ✓ Clarify the linkage and interfaces between work groups, e.g., operations, work planning, maintenance and engineering.

- ✓ Stimulate dialogue and action to improve performance both within the workgroup and improve its interfaces with other workgroups.

Ultimately, it is leaders who define the broader organizational purpose creating a clear and compelling picture of the organization's purpose and why its product or service is important. A high level, written purpose statement is a start. Leaders throughout the organization then personalize this purpose for each subgroup and individuals in those groups.

Once the organizational purpose is clear and each group's roles are clarified, the hard work begins. That is the collaboration among work groups to clarify their interfaces and dependencies for accomplishing the broader organizational goals. Again, it is valuable for the interdependent groups to define meaningful shared goals – an often-overlooked element of success.

Pervasive leadership is expressed when people throughout the organization take ownership for establishing these goals and refer to them in making hard decisions. Only then will other groups and managers be accountable for those decisions. It is one step in creating a healthy, performance driven culture.

There is another important concept we should consider in closing. What if you don't feel a compelling purpose? What if you don't have passion for your organization and the service it provides?

If you are a leader without a sense of purpose, it is time for a change. First, exercise your leadership skills to better define a truly meaningful purpose and gain support of others by applying the insights from this book. If that is not successful or you can no longer support your organization's purpose you need to change organizations. Our book, "*Career Aspirations*[5]" will be helpful in making these decisions.

Summary

Every organization has a purpose for existing, however, this purpose may not be clear and compelling to either the team members or the people it serves. This purpose is the foundation

---

[5] *Career Aspirations – Finding True Success in Your Career,* Bryce Shriver, et. al. available at Amazon.com

around which all other aspects of organizational success are built. It gives meaning to the team's unique and significant role.

A written purpose statement is a beginning but must become pervasive – providing guidance and energy to the organization. The value of a purpose statement is realized when it is personalized for individual work groups and integrated among work groups. This is accomplished by collaboration of those directly involved in the organization's work – not just those at the top of the organizational chart.

Application: Clarity of Purpose

1. What is your team's purpose - not in terms of what you do, but in terms of what you aspire to accomplish? How does it enrich the team members, the organization and society?

2. Collaborate with your team to clarify and strengthen its sense of purpose. Ask questions and actively listen to their responses over the course of a few weeks before attempting to develop or revise the written purpose statement.

3. Who do you need to collaborate with in other workgroups to clarify the interdependencies and establish mutual goals?

4. Consider how you can bring this purpose to life and encourage others to do the same. How can you relate it to your actions and the team's decisions each day? How do the others respond to your initiative?

"Brothers, I do not consider that I have made it on my own. But one thing I do: forgetting what lies behind and straining forward to what lies ahead, I press on toward the goal for the prize of the upward call of God in Christ Jesus."
Philippians 3:13-14 ESV[ii]

INTUITIVE, EFFECTIVE PROCESSES

Processes define how we will achieve our goals effectively and efficiently in a way that provides dignity for those who implement it.

Have you ever observed a clown car in a parade or, possibly, a goat rodeo? There is a great deal of activity but with no apparent purpose, organization or plan. It is fun to watch unless you are involved! Unfortunately, too many organizations operate as if every day was their first day – without the order and discipline needed to be either effective or efficient.

Our **purpose** defines both **what** we intend to accomplish and **why** it is worthy of our efforts. Our **process** defines **how** we will accomplish these goals effectively and efficiently and without the clowns or goats. Developing effective, efficient processes is one of the greatest values of *pervasive leadership.*

> *"Intuitive, effective processes ensure the quality of our product while respecting the individual – freeing them to accomplish those things that only people do well!"*

Defining a routine for our normal activities frees us up to do those things that only people do well, such as gaining wisdom from information, solving problems and developing positive relationships with others. These actions are vitally important to our success while busy work is a distraction from achieving our goals. Technology, properly applied, liberates us to perform these essential roles and avoid the mundane time killers.

Intuitive, effective processes are essential for organizational success. Without them we do not gain the full value of our efforts, we do not gain commitment from our team and we will not effectively support those who depend on our organization.

Ineffective processes create frustration and waste, while effective approaches multiply effectiveness, create enthusiasm and encourage us to apply our heart and mind, in addition to our hands, to achieve our goals.

Simply stated, a process is a series of steps taken to complete a task. It should have a logical sequence and will often be integrated with other activities that can be accomplished in parallel.

For example, we are all generally familiar with the assembly line process for building a car. Assembling an engine is a separate process, consisting of many steps, which merge with the basic structure of the car at the appropriate time on the assembly line. The same thoughts apply to other major components; body panels, interior components, wheels, etc. The goal is to bring all of the parts together, properly assembled and presented at the time needed to support the overall goal of providing a properly assembled, high quality vehicle.

It is easy to understand the importance and application of systematic processes in manufacturing, but what about other applications that perhaps require more flexibility? Does the concept of process apply to these applications that may have many decision points along the way?

The simple answer is yes. Consider sales, for example. A current advertisement for sales training states that 80% of sales presentations never ask for the customer to make a purchase. Doesn't it make sense to have a planned approach to sales that presents the benefits of the purchase, has prepared responses to customer questions and specifically asks for a decision?

The same concepts apply to a doctor's preparation for surgery, welcoming a new employee to your organization, repairing a computer or determining the needs of an individual approaching a social agency for help with a critical need. In each case, the objectives can be more effectively met by defining the needed steps.

An engineering or construction project is another example of this concept. Likewise, plans for meeting organizational goals can be developed as a logical sequence of actions.

The most common reason provided for not using a systematic process is that it would limit the needed flexibility. That is a symptom of a poorly developed process – one that does not consider potential problems and provides guidance for addressing them. This will be covered later, but it is a true advantage of having defined processes for most repetitive tasks.

"Strong processes multiply our effectiveness by committing our hearts and minds to those areas that are essential for success."

It is likely that your organization has a systematic approach for completing work, but do they meet the above definition? Do they engage you or are they viewed as an impediment to completing the task? Let's look at that more closely.

The first question we need to address is whether our processes are effective - assuring consistency and quality. Secondly, are the processes efficient, maximizing the value of our talents? Achieving these goals is a fundamental role of leaders and a clear reason for expanding the definition of our "leadership team". When *pervasive leadership* is present, many people become *process owners* committing their best efforts to ensure that the organization's goals are accomplished.

What are the attributes of an effective process? What is the best way to develop an efficient process or revise current processes that are too bureaucratic and cumbersome? These are key questions often asked when we are working with organizations to improve their performance.

> *"Two questions often arise concerning organizational processes:*
> - *What are the attributes of an effective process?*
> - *How can we develop this effective process?*

Let's address these two questions in turn.

Attributes of effective processes include:

- The process should define a logical sequence of repeatable steps that make sense to the individuals implementing it.

- Critical steps, those that must be performed correctly to ensure quality, should be clearly identified.

- Critical parameters and acceptance criteria should be clearly defined and verified.

- A parallel path of action should be included to cover cases where the acceptance criteria are not met. This element alone often pays rich rewards since it avoids confusion and wasted time.

- Interfaces among work groups should be well defined. For example, the organization having overall responsibility for the process and product should be defined.

- Routine, repetitive steps should be automated to the extent possible, freeing people to anticipate and resolve unexpected issues and ensure quality.

- Responsibility for completing each step should be well defined with particular emphasis on the support and transition among work groups.

- Where practical, contingency actions can be identified to be implemented if the process does not go as planned or required quality standards are not met. Collaboration in addressing these challenges should be encouraged.

- Processes can often be documented in simple flow charts with notations to identify critical steps, quality checkpoints and acceptance criteria. Additional detail may be provided in written procedures if needed.

Too often our processes are cumbersome, providing many administrative steps that do not create value and discourage innovation. Steps that don't add value should be eliminated – particularly bureaucratic reviews or approvals.

In one case, an essential quality attribute was not met but was signed off as being acceptable by five individuals.

Why did this happen?

For example, there was an important inspection of a critical component at a power plant that required five different reviews to verify acceptability. In one case, the acceptance criteria were not met, but the inspection was approved by all five individuals as being acceptable. When the error was identified, an expensive error, it was found that only one of the approvers had actually seen the test results but did not understand the acceptance criteria. The other four reviewers approved the test results assuming that the first reviewer was correct.

Why weren't the acceptance criteria and actual results clear? What value was there in having five reviewers? Those are questions that must be answered as the process is being developed.

How do we best establish or evaluate effective processes? The first principle is to involve those closest to the work – those who implement the process. It is also important to involve others who can ask tough questions concerning the logic and value of steps. Subject matter experts, individuals from interfacing organizations, knowledgeable and inexperienced workers as well as managers should be involved. Collaboration is the essential element.

As a starting point, gather a small group of employees to review one of your important but relatively simple processes. (Guidance on selecting the team is included in the chapter on Teamwork). This process review team should start by developing a simple flow chart (yes, a picture) of the process being evaluated. Once the high-level process flow chart is developed, the supporting sub-processes should be outlined with clarity of how and where they fit in the high-level process.

Once the simple flow chart is developed, the team will develop the details needed for successful implementation by considering these questions:

- What is the purpose of the process? What is the product or service? What are the essential attributes and quality standards?

- What are the essential steps that must be performed to achieve the goal? What groups are directly responsible for each step and what support is required by other groups?

- Does the process have checkpoints and acceptance criteria to ensure that the product has acceptable quality? If not, what are the missing attributes?

- Does the process identify the interfaces and transitions among work groups as necessary to keep the process moving while assuring quality? For example, in a work planning process, how are the required parts identified and procured to support the work group that will actually make the repair.

- Does the process define contingency actions or hold points if the required quality attributes are not met?

- When considering an existing process, it is important to ask if the process is actually implemented as defined by procedures? If not, why? Do employees take shortcuts to eliminate unneeded effort or add steps to ensure quality?

- Where are the "choke points", those places that limit the speed in which the product is provided? Are the choke points required to ensure quality? In some cases, these process restrictions result from limited resources or unneeded administrative burdens which can be resolved.

- How can technology be used to improve the effectiveness and efficiency of the process while freeing individuals to add value by evaluating the process and product?

- Does the process have unneeded steps? Does each step add value? Do quality inspections and approvals truly add value?

- Is the process understandable by a knowledgeable, intelligent person who was not involved in its development? Where do they question the value added by steps or requirements?

- What are the knowledge and skill required by individuals who will implement the process? What additional training is needed to ensure that the process is effective?

As noted, establishing effective, efficient processes is a key leadership function. There are at least five leadership roles in defining processes; namely,

- Defining the product and required attributes, such as, quality.

- Providing the organization and resources needed to implement the process. This includes defining the knowledge and skills of the individuals who will implement the process.

- Overseeing the process and product to ensure that it is effectively implemented and achieving the desired results. This includes collaborating with interfacing groups to ensure that transitions are effective.

- Resolving issues that inhibit process effectiveness or efficiency by making changes where needed. It should be noted that this is a commonly missed leadership role

- Encouraging collaboration to support innovation and process improvement, for example, the use of technology.

The first leadership role is directly tied to the organization's purpose. The broad purpose may include many sub-elements;

design, procurement, manufacturing, marketing, sales, etc. Yet, each of these sub-processes can be defined as a series of steps.

> *"In great organizations, the people closest to the actual work develop, implement and improve the work processes."*

Note that the first two roles are typically performed by people having traditional management positions and roles. The others can and should be performed by engaged employees who truly understand the process and its purpose. In fact, the most effective organizations are those where the people closest to the actual work have primary responsibility for monitoring and improving their processes.

The questions and actions noted above can be used to evaluate existing processes. It is particularly important to consider the *choke points*, those steps that require the most attention, and the interfaces where different organizations come together in the process.

Let's consider a simple example; A process for matching organizational volunteers to needed roles in a non-profit organization so that the needs of people being served are met. An example may be church ministry to meet the unique needs of single mothers in a low-income section of town. At a high level, this involves following, linked sub-processes:

Figure 1 Simple Process Flow Chart

```
┌─────────────────────────────────────────────────────────┐
│ Define the organization's purpose - its goals in terms  │
│ of who will be served and the specific needs to be met. │
└─────────────────────────────────────────────────────────┘
```

```
┌─────────────────────────────────────┐
│ Define the **process** for meeting  │
│ the needs of those served:          │
│                                     │
│ define the major actions needed to  │
│   achieve the purpose               │
│                                     │
│ develop a logical sequence and      │
│   grouping of steps                 │
│                                     │
│ Determine the number and location   │
│   of people needed to implement     │
│   the process.                      │
└─────────────────────────────────────┘
```

```
┌─────────────────────────────────────┐
│ Determine the technical skills,     │
│ interpersonal skills, temperament,  │
│ experience and interests of the     │
│ **volunteers** (see the chapter on  │
│ teamwork for approaches to defining │
│ individual skills and attributes)   │
└─────────────────────────────────────┘
```

```
┌─────────────────────────────────────┐
│ Systematically determine the        │
│ required and desired technical      │
│ skills, interpersonal skills and    │
│ experience needed to successfully   │
│ complete each grouping of steps in  │
│ the process.                        │
└─────────────────────────────────────┘
```

```
┌─────────────────────────────────────────────────────┐
│ Match potential volunteer skills and interests to   │
│ those required by the open positions.               │
│                                                     │
│ Define gaps in needed skills, desired skills and    │
│ volunteer interests.                                │
└─────────────────────────────────────────────────────┘
```

```
┌─────────────────────────────────────────────────────┐
│ Assign volunteers to fill open roles in the process.│
│                                                     │
│ Provide mentor & coach                              │
│                                                     │
│ Provide training to fill skill gaps                 │
│                                                     │
│ Provide real-time feedback                          │
└─────────────────────────────────────────────────────┘
```

Summary

The goals of an organization can be met through a series of logical steps defined as processes. The processes can be organized into logical sub-processes and the required actions, knowledge, skills and attributes required for their completion.

Effective processes are essential to success in most organizations since they help assure consistent quality, reduce costs and engage people in higher level activities where their experience and judgement add true value. Technology is used wisely to support these goals.

The best processes are intuitive, effective and efficient. This balance is best developed through collaboration among management, those who implement the process and those who support or interface with the process.

Process development is dynamic, always seeking improvement. The *pervasive leadership* model engages both formal and informal leaders in process improvement with the goal of enhancing both efficiency and quality on an on-going basis.

Application: Intuitive Effective Processes

1. Reflect on the concept of a process as a series of steps to achieve a goal logically and efficiently. Add your personal insights to develop a clear picture of an effective process.

2. Develop a simple diagram of the steps required to achieve a team goal. Clarify the critical steps - those that must be accomplished

as planned to achieve the desired goal. Add sub-elements under each critical step.

3. Highlight the steps that currently impede achieving the goal. Typically, these are interfaces among groups. Work with others to clarify how the process and interfaces should work and agree on actions to improve their effectiveness.

"Let all things be done decently and in order."
1 Corinthians 14:40. ESV

EXCEPTIONAL TEAMWORK

Teamwork: qualified, motivated individuals working together to achieve a worthy goal.

> "We organize to accomplish more than we can as individuals. It is only when we truly work together, with each individual contributing their unique and significant skills, that organizational magic flourishes."

If success were based on raw talent, the 2004 USA men's basketball team would have been awarded the Olympic gold medal without playing a game. The USA entry was often referred to as the "Dream Team". It included many of the of the NBA's upcoming stars; LeBron, Wade, Starbury, Duncan, and Iverson. In the end, teamwork overcame individual talent as the USA team suffered three losses including a 92-73 defeat by Puerto Rico, a commonwealth of only four million people. The team struggled to win the bronze metal and lost more games than the USA Olympic teams suffered in all previous Olympiads combined.

Teamwork often trumps talent both in sports and in more traditional organizations. But the unanswered question is why wasn't the teamwork developed? Isn't this an essential leadership role?

In the case of the 2004 Olympic team, the coaches undoubtedly attempted to make a team from well qualified players. What if the players themselves were committed to developing that teamwork? That is the essence of *pervasive leadership*.

> *"Pervasive Leadership in a team means that members of that team willingly seek to develop their team – to identify and resolve performance shortfalls instead of relying on those with management titles."*

Pervasive leadership is where individuals throughout the organization choose to lead instead of relying on those with formal manager titles. A fundamental prerequisite is that these potential leaders are qualified and sense their purpose as a part of a team – not as a lonely, sole contributor. We will start this quest by considering the factors that underlie teamwork that are easily transformed into *pervasive leadership*.

If, as discussed in earlier chapters, we have defined our purpose and the processes we use to accomplish our goals, it is time to consider who will do the actual work. Who, in terms of individuals and teams, will implement the processes to provide our products and services? As noted in the last chapter, defining the process requires that we consider the people that will implement it. Either we need to build the process around the team members' existing skills or develop the team's skills to match those demanded by the process.

> *"Leaders must invest their efforts in developing the team, not spending precious time writing policy and procedure manuals."*

Generally, both options should be melded, but in the end, the second approach is generally more viable. This requires a systematic approach - both in defining the required skill set and then selecting and developing the team members who will master these skills. Only then will our organization truly prosper. Yet this remains a major challenge since most organizations are not skilled in this essential role. Too often they spend more effort on developing policy manuals than they do on selecting and developing the teams upon which their success depends.

Consider the "job descriptions" in your organization. Is there a clear linkage between the specified job skills and those required to excel at the position and assure the organization's success?

Typically, the job requirements are stated in terms of education and experience. For example, a typical position requirement is a B.S. degree in engineering with six years of progressive experience. Perhaps, there is a bit more detail, such as, six years' experience in either automotive design engineering or test engineering. The questions not answered by this approach include true capability, ability to make decisions, resolve problems and bring out the best in others as a part of a team. In some cases, interpersonal skills and teamwork are considered during the hiring process, but often this occurs when people first enter the organization and not when considering people for specific career assignments.

Individual and team success depend on a host of interrelated attributes. Knowledge, skills and experience provide a foundation for completing the required tasks. There are other essential attributes, for example, interpersonal skills, initiative, judgment and the ability to manage stress. Aren't these important team skills? The players on the 2004 men's Olympic basketball team had greater ability than those they played against, yet they played as individuals and lost.

We won't discuss the theory of teamwork - that is generally well understood. Instead, we focus on three interrelated aspects of teamwork and the leadership roles in developing them. Two of these aspects are *commitment* and *culture*. These are covered in the following chapters. The third is matching and developing team member skills, including communications and judgement, to the process needs. That is the major item to be explored in this chapter.

One important role of a leader is to evaluate these broader attributes and then select and develop the team to truly meet the demands of the process. The leader's role is to meld them – to both improve the process and develop the team responsible for implementation. Again, this role is not limited to those holding a management title.

> *"The capability of the individuals and teams must match those required by the process they will implement.*
>
> *Too often, we only consider the technical skills while temperament and attitude are just as important."*

In most cases, we are not starting from nothing with either the process or the team that will implement it. Success demands that we integrate the two; yet this is rarely done in a systematic way. Assuming that the process is reasonably well defined, let's explore the individual and team attributes that are essential for its effective implementation by considering the following areas:

- *Technical knowledge* – basic understanding of the technology and business. Often provided through education or formal training, for example in engineering, accounting, electronics or sales contracts.

- *Skills* - capability to perform physical and mental tasks, such as repairing a computer, evaluating a design change or analyzing data to determine tax liability. These skills also result from the application of training and experience.

- *Personality or temperament* - ability to demonstrate effective interpersonal skills and teamwork. Examples include listening to understand differing ideas and views, the ability to translate ideas into meaningful actions and demonstrating social awareness. While many of these attributes are inherent, they can be developed as well.

- *Judgement & problem solving* – ability to understand higher level reasoning, make sound decisions, solve complex problems, develop alternative approaches, evaluate unintended consequences of decisions and manage stress when things don't go as planned.

- *Attitude and passion* - intrinsic desire to serve in the required roles resulting in commitment of discretionary effort to add value. This will be covered in the next chapter.

That is a daunting list. Consider the value in having leaders throughout the organization help in defining and developing these items.

With that in mind, let's develop a few of these in more detail:

Knowledge and Skills

Knowledge and skills can be defined and developed using a systematic approach such as that defined by Bloom's[6] taxonomy of learning. This process includes the systematic review of the tasks, processes and technology to determine the required knowledge and skills as the basis for developing training to provide the needed competencies.

A simple starting point is to gather a group of experienced, high performing team members with an educational technologist to develop a listing of the required skills. Key leadership roles include ensuring that this summary is accurate and relevant. Second, leaders support implementation of the training to assure that the incumbents benefit from it. People are more committed and successful when their knowledge and skills match those required by the job.

Experience is developed by actively engaging team members in all phases of the process, including resolution of process and quality problems. It is expanded through temporary assignments to other interfacing groups. Learning is enhanced by aligning the individuals with highly experienced mentors and assuring a wide range of experiences.

---

[6] www.en.wikipedia.org/wiki/bloom's-taxonomy

The specific skills should be optimized within the team. For example, consider the mix of craft personnel in the maintenance group of a factory. While all may have excellent basic skills, some will likely focus on mechanical components while others focus on electrical systems or control systems. Even within these areas there will likely be sub-specialties. The question is whether we have the optimum distribution of skills to meet the work requirements.

Defining the needed knowledge and skills is essential in developing *pervasive leadership.* Having the requisite skills forms a basis for assessing better ways to complete the job and find their place on the team.

Personality or Temperament

Personality or temperament are also important. There are many personality profiles that are useful for helping individuals and organizations develop stronger teams. The Myers Briggs Type Indicator[7] (MBTI) is one useful example. The MBTI describes our temperament in terms of preferences that affect our behavior patterns. For example, are we energized by people or by thoughts and ideas? Do we make decisions quickly or do we like to keep our options open? Are we energized or drained by being with a group of people?

---

[7] www.meyersbriggs.org and Please Understand Me II, by David Keirsey, Prometheus Nemesis Book Company, 1998

In this model, there are sixteen different preference groupings although, in reality, it is a continuum among four groups of differing preferences. Let's see how this concept applies to teamwork.

- Consider a team role that requires a strong focus on reviewing objective data to verify that key product attributes are met and identify adverse trends using a "rules based" approach. Someone with an introspective, detailed, objective decision-making temperament is a good match. In MBTI terminology, an ISTJ fits this role well.

- In a second example, consider a person who coordinates work among three different workgroups to resolve emergent problems. There is a wide range of emergent problems with differing priorities and a varying mix of skills needed for their resolution. As a result, the ability to optimize the assignment of resources from different work groups will be more important than in the prior example. The ability to see the bigger picture, assign priorities and develop flexible approaches is likely required - a MBTI ENTP may be well suited to this role.

- Now consider the implications for reversing these roles. The ENTP people-oriented communicator who seeks options and possibilities will likely struggle with a detailed, objective data analysis job. Likewise, the ISTJ will likely struggle with the lack of definition and ever-changing priorities of the workgroup coordinator role. Both roles are essential, but the best value comes from matching the natural temperament to the job demands.

- Another application considers the role of temperament in assigning work to technicians who, in theory, have the same skills. Yet, some will likely have temperaments more suited to trouble shooting which requires higher level diagnostic skills as compared to another person who is better suited to routine surveillances where the objective is to evaluate and calibrate equipment to defined standards.

In summary, it is important to understand and properly apply these concepts in developing effective teams. There are several web-based tools to help in this important quest.[8]

How does this support developing *pervasive leadership*? It is not by trying to fit everyone into the classic ENTJ or ESTJ boxes that leaders typically exhibit. Instead, proper implementation of temperament allows us to encourage leadership from those who do not relish being out-front.

Consider an introverted individual who cherishes time to explore and develop ideas alone. Providing time and provocative questions may encourage that individual to take a leadership role in improving processes or addressing problems. Likewise, someone with a strong connection to people (MBTI with a high feeling score) may be more likely to express their concerns with the impact of business decisions by the classic ESTJ if consistently asked for insights from those ESTJ's in formal leadership positions.

---

[8] e.g., www.bestfittype.com

Judgement and Problem Solving

Another important, yet often overlooked, aspect of teamwork is sound judgement and problem solving. This is usually developed through experience.

"Good judgement is largely developed through experience – active learning from the prior bad judgment of ourselves and others are the path to this rare commodity."

This is another area where *pervasive leadership* pays rich dividends. When people throughout the organization apply their unique experience and skill, problems are typically solved quickly and with quality that lasts. In organizations where top-down leadership prevails much of the team is idle while the big guys debate the issue and often miss its underlying causes.

On the other hand, how often have you seen management pull a team together to address a valid issue only to find the team to be ineffective? Application of High Impact Teams (HIT), cross-functional teams, etc. is valid, but only if properly implemented.

Based on our experience, there are several important actions needed to gain value from the *collaboration* of these teams. These include:

- Clearly defining the problem in terms of its scope and importance. Too often the scope of the issue is ill-defined, not providing the clarity needed for the team.

- Optimizing the team composition. It is essential to include individuals closest to the problem with their wealth of practical experience, however, these individuals often have a limited paradigm that hinders their ability to see innovative solutions. There is value in including people with process knowledge but not directly responsible for the specific area being addressed. Examples include individuals from other organizations that interface with the process being evaluated, millennial generation team members who have strong social awareness and technical savvy as well as the classic subject matter experts. The objective is to gain the value of collective intelligence – bringing differing perspectives and experiences to the problem. Typically, five to ten members is optimum since this allows diversity of experience while encouraging each member to fully participate.

- Ensuring constructive interaction among team members. Social perceptiveness of team members – the ability to read the emotions and insights of others – should be among the key selection criteria for team members. It is this social awareness that forms the foundation of "collective intelligence". The value of using a group is only realized by encouraging active participation by all team members to develop solutions that may not otherwise be explored. Generally, this requires face-to-face meetings where emotions can be expressed and spontaneous discussion encouraged.

- Providing management support. Line leaders have three important roles; namely; assure that the problem is properly defined, help assure that the broader implications of proposed solutions are considered and actively support implementation of the recommendations. These roles are often overlooked. Successful implementation of recommendations often requires a *champion* with leadership skills and authority to address the normal organizational reluctance to implement meaningful change.

- Evaluating the cost of implementation, both in financial and human impact terms. This includes a robust review of potential *unintended consequences*. It is important to include individuals on the team who provide these perspectives.

Effective use of teams to resolve problems is a hallmark of leadership. Including individuals with strong technical skills, inquisitive minds and adequate interpersonal skills in this collaborative mission is an important step in developing *pervasive leadership*.

The First-Line Supervisor and Pervasive Leadership

Let's return to the concept of *pervasive leadership*. There is often a need for a catalyst to develop true teamwork even when team members have the needed skills. That catalyst is often the first-line supervisor.

Supervisors are the bridge; defining the goals and expectations of managers for the people who must actually achieve them. Are these supervisors selected based on their ability to communicate and encourage commitment? Do they reinforce each other when applying performance expectations or rewarding high performance? Are they developed as a team and provided development opportunities to assure that they are capable of performing their supervisory role comfortably, gaining the respect of all those they serve?

> *"The first-line supervisor is the often overlooked catalyst for developing exceptional teamwork!"*

In addition, are first-line supervisors encouraged to apply *pervasive leadership* concepts within their team? It is typically the first-line supervisor who can encourage the connection between their team's role and the broader organizational goals, enable team members to evaluate and enhance their processes and identify needed skill enhancements.

This leads to the question of how we develop the first line supervisors' skills and temperament discussed in this chapter? A strong first step is by leading them in a discussion of this chapter and encouraging their insights on how to develop the concepts in the larger organization and in their work group. I have been amazed at how quickly this approach has transformed an organization from hierarchical leadership model to a *pervasive leadership* approach.

Collaboration is the goal of each of the elements discussed. The value of any team is found in their ability to rely on each other's strengths to create a synergy of ideas, abilities and outcomes. It is when these individual factors are melded that success is assured. At its heart, teamwork is about collaboration.

Summary

The leader's role is to understand the valid job requirements in terms of technical skills, attitudes and temperament and then select and develop individuals to fill these roles. Attributes that should be evaluated in this quest include:

- Technical knowledge and skills

- Personality or temperament

- Judgement & Problem solving

- Attitude & passion (to be developed in following chapters)

Where leadership is pervasive, this responsibility is actively pursued throughout the organization. Individuals and teams throughout the organization will look at both the process and existing talent to find ways to improve performance.

This selection and development process can become a highly constructive, energizing experience as people sense that they truly fit in the organization and their contribution is valued. Work loses its negative connotation when people are using their skills and natural abilities in achieving a worthy goal, particularly when they see their leadership influence have a positive impact on the team.

The goal of these concepts is to develop a team where collaboration is the norm – where individuals contribute their individual skills while welcoming the input, effort and leadership of others. The value of the team is in multiplying the effectiveness of its individual members.

Application: Exceptional Teamwork

1. What are the collective knowledge, skills and attitudes required to achieve your team's goals? Consider the education, experience and personality profiles that best meet these needs.

2. Understand your personality - your individual preferences, strengths and gaps - to gain an understanding of how you can best serve the team. Specifically, gain insights concerning your social awareness and ability to draw out the best in others.

3. Consider your team. What are its most prominent strengths? What weaknesses challenge its performance? What opportunities exist to strengthen the team and its contribution? What threatens to make the team ineffective? How can you, individually and as a team, strengthen performance?

4. Consider how you can promote collaboration by helping the team identify and resolve a long-standing performance concern. Establish a clear framework where each individual contributes based on their experience and temperament.

"For by the grace given to me I say to everyone among you not to think of himself more highly than he ought to think, but to think with sober judgment, each according to the measure of faith that God has assigned. For as in one body, we have many members, and the members do not all have the same function, so we, though many, are one body in Christ, and individually members one of another. Having gifts that differ according to the grace given to us,
let us use them..."
Romans 12:3-6 ESV

COMMITMENT TO ORGANIZATIONAL SUCCESS

Individually placing the organization's success above our personal desires

"Commitment to a cause is a deeply held value, one that is intrinsic, not motivated by lectures but through deeply held beliefs. It is this intrinsic power that unleashes the best we have to offer."

"We are preparing to shut the plant down since it is not clear we can repair the transformer in the allowed time," the site manager told me.

I was four states away attending an industry conference and had earlier asked about the electrical transformer repair plans and status. There had been little clarity about contingency plans if the direct repair was unsuccessful. The transformer was a regulatory requirement since it provided power to critical systems, but there were options both for the repair and for alternate power supplies.

Now, as I was ready to board the plane for the return trip, it appeared that all other options had been set aside. Shutting the plant down was now the "plan" since it was unknown how long it would take to obtain replacement parts.

Shutting down the plant was no minor decision. While we would not hesitate to do so if there was a safety concern, it was costly in terms of the impact on employees' personal lives and the direct loss of over two million dollars of revenue each day.

I called again when I arrived at my home airport, hoping for a more optimistic report. There was not one. Again, it was not clear that robust alternatives were being considered. I requested that the leadership team meet with me in an hour. The site manager was not enthusiastic about my request, so the expectation was clarified – the time, location and attendees specified.

Upon arriving at the plant, my first stop was at the transformer – the place where repairs were being made. But they weren't – no one was there. I went to the electrical shop, assuming that they were calibrating the electrical components which were the source of the problem. I found only two electricians – they were awaiting the work package and parts but did not know when either would arrive. The story was similar when I talked with the work planners and warehouse crew – no one knew the actual status and there was no clear path to success.

When I arrived at the meeting room, only half of the key leaders were there. The others had gone home hours ago, before the extent of the problem was known. It was, after all, Friday. The status report I received from the managers was not accurate – not reflecting the information I had received from the people who were actually doing the work. In the end, we shut the plant down – I had only added frustration.

Ownership, commitment? Where were they? Where had I failed? How had a large organization, including well qualified leaders, accepted defeat so readily? Why had they not pursued multiple approaches to resolving the equipment problem? Why didn't they see the importance of fixing the issue before shutting the plant down?

Have you experienced a similar situation? Have you seen an urgent, important need for action that was not shared by your organization? Have you wondered why there was no sense of urgency in addressing needs and wondered how you can change the outcome?

Once again, developing *pervasive leadership* was the answer. Once individuals throughout the plant embraced their unique leadership roles that sense of commitment thrived.

> *"Commitment comes from within. It comes when we have emotional, intellectual and spiritual values that are connected to our organization's purpose."*

Commitment comes from within. It is ownership of the result – it is being driven to achieve something that we personally value – not just giving a half-hearted effort. That ownership rarely comes from external urging. It is a result of individuals' emotional, intellectual and spiritual values being connected to the goal – the organization's purpose developed in the earlier chapter.

It is easy to assume that we have a common understanding of commitment. Yes, we generally know it when it is present, but what are the behaviors we see? How can we objectively evaluate our commitment or that of other members of our team? Here are some tangible indicators of strong commitment:

- Placing a high priority on organizational success even when conflicting with our personal comfort or risk aversion.

- Having an emotional response to the organization's performance, much like our response to our favorite sports team winning or losing an important game.

- Investing our personal time and energy in the quest for success, for example, thinking of how we can improve the group's performance while on vacation.

- Actively seeking new approaches to improving performance even when it is outside our experience or comfort zone.

- Discussing the organization and its success with friends and acquaintances.

- Supporting others to achieve organizational goals even if it detracts from our personal or group's accomplishments.

- Demonstrating high levels of personal behavior and integrity, believing that our example will affect others' view the organization.

So, the question becomes how do we develop these values in individuals so that it permeates the organization? Developing ownership and commitment is a leadership function that comes naturally when *pervasive leadership* is present.

We start by internalizing the organization's purpose – explaining with intellectual and emotional rigor what we are to accomplish and why it is important. As expressed earlier, it is essential that this purpose is linked to individuals and their teams so we all understand and feel the importance of those goals.

The quest continues by clarifying our unique and significant role in accomplishing the goals. We must believe that what we are doing has real value. We need a picture of success and our personal and team's essential role in completing that portrait and, with its accomplishment, a sense of personal victory.

> *"Commitment is gained only when we, as leaders, demonstrate commitment and personally request it from others in a compelling way."*

The leader is the team's coach – the one explaining, showing, and demonstrating the importance of the organization's achievement. It also requires us to express how the team and organization will be affected if we fail. Our role is to inspire that sense of personal and corporate pride. It is an integral part of the encouraging culture that we will discuss in the next chapter.

Note that we refer to leaders, not managers based on an organizational chart. Just as the offensive unit of a football team is inspired by individuals on the defense, we are compelled to seek success when it is actively promoted by our peers.

This is an essential element of *pervasive leadership*. Success is only achieved when a "critical mass" of leaders in each team, each group and the organization as a whole understand the importance of what we are to achieve and are personally committed to achieving it.

> *"Collaboration is the essential ingredient in achieving true, lasting success. Are you the leader that facilitates this essential element?"*

Encouraging collaboration is essential in the quest for widespread commitment to the organization's success. Collaboration is expressed when individual team members step in to assure the team's success – even when it's not their direct responsibility. It's when members of one team reach across organizational boundaries to improve the interfaces – to cover the gaps or weaknesses in the processes.

It is a leader's role to develop this ownership in others by:

- ✓ Emphasizing the individual's and the team's unique and essential role in achieving the organizational goal in clear compelling ways – touching their mind, heart and spirit.

- ✓ Demonstrating personal commitment to achieving the goals – visibly and overtly. The purpose is two-fold; to reinforce the importance of the organizational goal and to exhibit the actions, values and commitment required to achieve it.

- ✓ Asking the individuals and team how we can accomplish the goal. Ask about the barriers, the obstacles that are inhibiting their ability to achieve the goal. You will be amazed at their insights. Act on them – removing barriers that were identified is an essential step in building commitment.

- ✓ Personally, asking for support and commitment from the team and team members. As a starting point, pick some important event or goal where you can make the request for commitment clear, specific and personal. Ask for support and some tangible expression of their support. Gaining a tangible expression of commitment is important – we are much more likely to meet our obligations if we have personally agreed to support them.

- ✓ Encouraging collaboration among those most involved in the situation. This comes as we ask questions concerning who should be involved in the decisions and seek their insights.

- ✓ Celebrate successes – recognize team accomplishments in ways that are meaningful to the group. We will discuss this more in the next chapter.

Yes, this is a tough order. It is not easy to truly follow these steps – your personal commitment is required. Yet, why do we expect others to be truly committed if we, as leaders, are not? We do not respond to "broadcast" requests for support, why should our team? Personal involvement, making the need real and relevant, is essential.

The important point is that as we model these steps, we encourage others to do the same even before we ask.

This process works. It was applied to address the "bad day" example discussed in an earlier chapter. We started by assuring that the organizational goals were clearly stated – they were pictured in the form of a puzzle with each piece representing a key goal. When combined, the puzzle presented a beautiful picture of our plant – our success.

We discussed these goals and their importance in small group meetings where the specific support needed from that group was debated. Barriers were identified and multi-discipline teams collaborated to find the best solutions.

As a part of this process each employee was asked, personally, for their commitment and to signify it by placing their thumb print (yes – using an ink pad to put their thumbprint on the poster that was then placed in a prominent location) on the upcoming challenge – the "big event" that would determine our success for the year.

We were successful! In every respect we achieved and excelled. We won 43 to 0. And we celebrated!

> *"Passion, and the creativity it breeds, comes with accomplishing worthy goals - by seeing that our efforts drive the organization, helping those it serves!"*

That was the start of a new path – one that led to success for several years. Developing commitment – intrinsic ownership – is hard, but absolutely worth the investment. It is a key step in building *pervasive leadership* and a constructive culture.

Let's return to the role of *pervasive leadership*. Formal leaders must demonstrate their commitment before it flourishes throughout the organization. These leaders must demonstrate passion for success as shown by:

- ✓ Relentlessly reinforcing the organization's purpose in meaningful ways while sharing the importance of each individual and group in achieving the goals.

- ✓ Being present and encouraging collaboration when things are not going as planned. The simple act of asking those closest to the work for insights and acting on them encourages their initiative and, with it, leadership in anticipating and resolving issues before they become a crisis.

- ✓ Openly acknowledging those who contribute to meeting the organization's goals while avoiding the natural tendency to find fault.

Being present and constructively involved is the key ingredient in this quest. Asking questions, removing barriers and focusing on success set the leadership example that will be adopted by individuals.

> *"Our individual commitment to the organization's success is strengthen when our personal aspirations are being fulfilled."*

As we close this chapter, there is one more important element in building commitment within an organization. That is fulfilling the personal aspirations of team members. When each person's intrinsic desires are met, they naturally have a commitment to the organization.

Collectively, we have found that those who contribute most to the organization and find deep, inner satisfaction - share six **Career Aspirations**. These are:

- ✓ A strong sense of **belonging** - of being a welcomed and respected part of a team.

- ✓ A clear sense of **purpose and accomplishment** driven by a deep, inner passion, to accomplish goals bigger than a single individual can achieve.

- ✓ A positive view of the **future** – an encouraging expectation of personal development, opportunity and rewards.

- ✓ An energizing **respect** for the **organization** they serve and **those who lead it**.

- ✓ An abundance of meaningful **rewards**, both tangible and intangible.

- ✓ A healthy **life balance** – developing meaningful relationships and interests beyond the career while living consistent with our values.

In addition to these six aspirations there are at least two cross-cutting attributes that underlie our sense of well-being: namely, **personal respect** and **autonomy**. These aspirations are developed in our book, **Career Aspirations**[9] which includes insights on how these attributes can be developed.

Summary

While true commitment comes from within, it is often inspired by other leaders who, through their personal passion, connect with the hearts and minds of others. It comes when a positive spirit of collaboration extends throughout the organization. Success is ensured when this passion is actively expressed and rewarded.

Dr. Travis Bradbury[10] describes this commitment as "grit" stating that is the passion, perseverance and stamina that we must channel in order to stick with our dreams until they become a reality. Dr. Bradbury's signs of grit are summarized as:

You Have Grit If You...

- ✓ Make mistakes, look like an idiot and then try again without flinching.

- ✓ Fight when you already feel defeated.

- ✓ Make calls (decisions) that you are afraid to make.

- ✓ Keep your emotions in check.

- ✓ Trust your gut without being impulsive.

---

[9] Bryce Shriver, et. al., Career Aspirations – Finding True Success in Your Career, ©2022 by Three Seven Research, Inc. Available at www.Amazon.com
[10] Do You Have Grit by Dr Travis Bradbury. www.linkedin.com/pulse/do-you-have-grit-dr-Travis-Bradbury

- ✓ Give more than you get in return.

- ✓ Lead when no one else follows.

- ✓ Meet deadlines that are unreasonable while delivering results that exceed expectations.

- ✓ Focus on important details even when it makes your mind numb.

- ✓ Are kind to people who are rude to you.

- ✓ Are accountable for your actions, no matter what.

How do we avoid quitting when success does not come easily? How do we remain energized and focused on accomplishing greatness when we face seemingly unending challenges? Perseverance combined with technical skills, interpersonal skills and judgement is the answer. There is no short cut.

Application: Commitment to Organizational Success

1. Rate your team's commitment to achieving the organization's goals using a 0 to 5 scale. Zero indicates a lack of commitment, three is marginally acceptable and five is a strong commitment. What are the indications of strong or weaker commitment?

2. Evaluate the contributors to areas of strong commitment in terms of the *Seven Characteristics of Successful Organizations* summarized at the end of the "A Leadership Crisis" chapter. Do the same for areas lacking commitment.

3. Evaluate your personal commitment to the organization's success. Would a knowledgeable outsider rate your commitment as one, three or five? What objective evidence would they cite in making this assessment? Explore these conclusions in terms of the leadership principles discussed in prior chapters.

4. Discuss the concept of commitment with others in your group. Use the *Seven Characteristics of Successful Organizations* and the concepts in this chapter to collaborate to identify ways to enhance and reward individual and organizational commitment.

"Whatever you do, work heartily, as for the Lord and not for men, knowing that from the Lord you will receive the inheritance as your reward. You are serving the Lord Christ."
Colossians 3:23-24. ESV

INNOVATION AND RENEWAL

Growing and adapting to meet the demands of our ever-changing world

"True leaders welcome change, it's the old, the obsolete and ineffective that they fear, knowing that these are the very things that lead to demise!"

In today's world, success requires change! Innovation is essential in building our organization whether it is a university, business or non-profit organization. Many of today's economy cars outperform the beloved 60's "muscle cars" in braking, handling and fuel economy. Would you trade your smart phone for a rotary, land line phone that costs a quarter a minute for calls across the city? How about the hand calculator bought in the 1970's for the price of today's basic tablet computer? Just like obsolete products, organizations and processes must be renewed to incorporate advances in technology and society.

"Change is the most difficult challenge most organizations face, yet few will thrive without continual renewal of their products, technologies and processes."

Clinging to the past may seem romantic, but very few organizations excel for more than a decade without innovation - without renewing their products, processes and technology.

Consider the change in retail marketing during the 21st century. Earlier, there was concern with the impact that K-Mart® and

Walmart® were having on local, family-owned businesses. Now K-Mart is a memory and Walmart is losing business to Amazon® which only began as a book seller late in the last century. Likewise, the U.S. Postal Service lost business to UPS® and FedEx® which are now being challenged by Amazon Prime's vast shipping network.

Consider our financial system. Fifty years ago, cash was king. We quickly moved to credit cards and other forms of electronic payments. Today, cryptocurrencies are invading our system with the possibility of making cash and the federally controlled financial system obsolete. Our lives and our organizations must change if we are to survive.

Yet, change is the most difficult challenge for most organizations to master. We, along with organizations, inherently seek stability. It provides a sense of security - we know the rules and have developed competency. Often, both we and our organization have been successful with the current process and seem to forget the many changes that occurred over the years.

Take a moment to ponder that premise - what has changed in your organization? Look back a decade. Are you in the same position, working with the same people? Are your products or services the same? Are you using the same computer and software? Is your interface with those you serve the same? Are the regulatory and administrative requirements the same? How about the customers you serve - have their expectations remained stagnant? Have you been required to learn new skills as a result of all of these changes?

An important role of leaders is to seek opportunity to improve. The most fundamental change is to provide our current services better, faster and cheaper. The goal is to serve more people while reducing the cost and improving the quality. Secondly, there is a need to offer new products and services. Lastly, change is desirable to free individuals and organizations from monotonous tasks that do not require the intellectual, emotional and moral aspects of the human spirit.

There are generally two reasons for change; innovation and adaptation. For example, advances in technology often bring increased productivity and quality, but do not fundamentally change our purpose or processes. In other cases, demographic and social changes require adaptation to provide new products, services or approaches.

A second way of looking at change is by considering the extent and impact of the change. Changes are typically evolutionary, incremental steps in response to changes in technology or societal needs. In other cases, it can be transformational – dramatically changing our product or process.

For example, consider the application of technology which has led to fundamental changes in the way we share world events. Twitter®, Facebook® and YouTube® now provide instant access to world events where just a decade before we relied on traditional news reporters and camera crews. Likewise, several years ago land-line internet connections were heralded as the source of information. Now smart phones and smart watches negate the need for obsolete desk-top computers.

How we classify changes is not important. The important mind set is to look for the need and opportunity to change. We do this by listening to those we serve and to our team. We must analyze our processes and evaluate the value of our product. We seek the opportunity to broaden our service and apply innovative approaches that are transferred from other organizations or made possible by new technology. It is an ongoing process – one enhanced when *pervasive leadership* is present.

> *"The most Successful Leaders are Outliers[11] – they do things differently than the other Leaders within their industry. They are trailblazers and non-conformists."*

> *"Industry insiders do things the same way everyone else within their industry does things. They toe the line and conform to rules, protocols, strategies and industry guidelines. They do what everyone else before them did. They are cautious and adverse to taking risks."*

Change and innovation must occur, that is not the debate. The real question is does the change improved the product and process? A deeper question is whether you are engaged in the change, helping define the desired outcomes, considering the potential "unintended

---

[11] https://richhabits.net/leadership-series-common-traits-of-successful-leaders-trait-14-outlier-mindset/

consequences" and evaluating the benefits once the change was implemented?

In the *pervasive leadership* model, the answer to both of these questions is yes. Not every employee needs to be involved in every change. Yet, if you are affected by a major change in an organization with a *pervasive leadership* culture you will likely participate, making the change viable and achieving the overall goals.

How do we identify the need and develop the plan for innovation or process improvement? Secondly, how does *pervasive leadership* enhance these changes?

We start with a clear statement of the existing condition by asking what is working and what is not effective in meeting the organization's goals? Once potential areas for improvement are identified it is important to assess their importance and cause. Once the underlying needs for change are understood we can start working to develop and implement the needed changes.

- When the need for change is driven by poor performance, it is good to look within. Encourage collaboration among peer leaders to ask what worked in the past? What similar processes are working well in other parts of the organization?

- When the purpose of the change is to improve effectiveness and efficiency it is often best to assemble a team to review the process. Begin by looking at the delays, those places that tend to inhibit the flow of work or require excessive intervention. Listen to the leaders closest to the work - where are their challenges, frustrations and bottlenecks? They will often have the solution.

- When process or quality challenges have been clearly defined, it is beneficial to seek insights from our peers in other organizations. Typically, they have faced similar challenges and developed solutions that we can adopt and enhance.

- If the need for change is driven by changes in technology, there may be a need for assistance from outside the organization to consider the challenges and implications.

- Another approach is to seek insights from unrelated industries. For example, many insights concerning flight crew dynamics developed by the airline industry were applied to operational crews at nuclear power plants.

The key in all cases is to challenge the existing paradigm. This generally requires that we look outside our work group and organization. Again, the role of the leader is first to identify the need for improvement - to recognize that frustration, delays and poor quality are generally a cry for innovation, not a sign of laziness or apathy. Where there is *pervasive leadership*, the recognition of and creative solutions for resolving these challenges come from within the organization.

To excel, leaders must be systematic in their approach to change. They must address the following aspects of any significant change:

- Benefit - clear definition of the purpose and value of the change.

- Magnitude - involvement of those closest to the change to define its breadth and depth.

- Cost - direct and indirect impacts on others. Unintended consequences must be considered and addressed.

- Risks – determine what can go wrong and the consequences of failure. Compensatory measures should be established to minimize both the probability and consequences of these failures.

- Implementation plan - integration of each of the above considerations into actionable steps and controls.

- Lastly, potential unintended consequences must be considered and addressed. This is an often-underemphasized step in the change process – one that may negate the value of the proposed change.

Pervasive leadership energizes identification and implementation of changes in each of these steps. While those closest to the work may not initially see the problem, they are usually best equipped to make changes once the need is clear.

Leaders must accept some risk of failure; not all "improvements" work. While not desirable, failure is acceptable if it is not too costly and leads to deeper understanding that will be applied in the future.

How do we avoid costly failure? There are several methods that work well in the *pervasive leadership* model. The most important is to involve "thought leaders" from throughout the organization – those individuals who are known for questioning decisions and considering options. Listen carefully as they explore what needs to change and who will be affected, both directly and indirectly. Then systematically review potential unintended consequences of the change and define the worst possible outcome. Then establish monitoring and controls so that compensatory actions can be taken to identify and correct adverse conditions before they become significant.

Here is a challenging example; namely, differing approaches to staff reduction at two similar, large businesses. In both cases, the application of technology, improved work processes and gains in employees' skills and motivation resulted in more people than were needed to accomplish the company goals. In each case, the employees filling the unneeded positions were treated with respect and provided with similar good severance benefits. That is where the similarity ended.

- In the first case, targeted reductions were established by senior management. The decision was made to only seek volunteers willing to leave the organization in return for the severance benefits. This sounds like a great approach - right? It was not. The unintended consequences were profound. For example:

    o Most who left were high performing employees, newly hired engineers and well qualified technicians who had no problem in finding similar positions and enjoyed the "free money" as they pursued their new career. Fortunately, many great employees remained

– those who had built their career with us and were intensely loyal to our organization.

    o Less fortunate was that many low performance employees remained - those with limited job skills and initiative.

    o Another weakness of this approach was that it did not consider the workload within each group or the potential loss of critical experience.

Collectively, this approach to staff reduction increased the workload and frustration of the many good employees who remained.

- In the second company, the separation process was selective with a combination of volunteers and targeted resignations. The need for change and the selection process were clearly defined. Reduction targets were established by considering the work process, not solely by budgets. Leaders throughout the organization engaged in selecting the individual's leaving the organization and to assure that the right people and skills were retained. They actively involved the employees selected for retention in revising their processes to reflect the leaner organization which emphasized the importance of the new team in the organization's future. Both performance and morale improved.

A key reason for the success in the second example was providing a clear focus on the organization's purpose and the application of *pervasive leadership* principles. By involving people throughout the organization in the need for these changes, the benefits of improving processes and teamwork were realized. In addition, the impact of the changes was considered and steps taken to ensure that they were constructive.

In most cases, changes are evolutionary and can be managed to gain their value. Sometimes, however, transformational change is needed. The challenge of major changes associated with true renewal or fundamental change in our products, processes or services is far greater than simple process improvements. These are changes to our fundamental business, products or approach. For example, electrical utilities desired to move into land development, communications, and emerging markets in the late 1990's. Nearly all failed.

Likewise, renewal is not easy. It is often hard to see the need for change or welcome the unsettling feeling it brings. Often there is frustration and inefficiency associated with change leading us to question whether the change is worth the cost, particularly when it is not well developed and impact on other organizational aspects is not considered.

How do we minimize the risk of transformational change? We start by clarifying the scope of the change and its anticipated benefits. Only then can we begin a systematic review by answering fundamental questions, such as:

- Do we have the experience and expertise to ensure success?

- Does it add to or build on our current core competence?

- What is our core competency that the change builds on?

- Do we understand the new product or service?

- Why are we better equipped to undertake this change than other organizations with similar interests and capability? What makes us the best organization to pursue this opportunity?

- Does it require renewal of skills and approaches for both the team and the individual?

- Does it change our basic mission or purpose, risking loss of focus?

- Does it increase our risk in a way that may adversely affect our core business? For example, what are the costs in terms of finances, reputation, etc.?

- Does it distract key leaders and resources from our current, successful endeavors?

When leaders throughout the organization participate in these evaluations the probability of success is much higher. These leaders can ensure the changes are well developed and that impact on other parts of the organization is considered. Leaders question change, not to block it, but to make certain that it is well planned and adds value.

Summary

In the end, change is inevitable. The leader's role is to ensure that the change is truly an improvement - that it adds value. Constant change leads to frustration and loss of focus.

The key challenge is to clearly identify the need for change by examining the underlying conditions. While those most involved in the processes being evaluated may not recognize the change, they are often the most qualified to help design and implement the change.

By implementing the *pervasive leadership* model, the organization will welcome innovation and the true value it brings.

Application: Innovation and Renewal

1. Consider the process weakness you evaluated in the chapter on that topic. Reach out to an innovative team member to gain insights into how technology can improve the process.

2. Conduct an exercise with a broad-based group of team members to consider how your product or process should be transformed to meet the challenges of the 21st century.

3. Take action to broaden your perspective or skills. For example, complete an assessment of your leadership style and effectiveness using one of the profiles referenced in the following chapter.

"Do not be conformed to this world, but be transformed by the renewal of your mind, that by testing you may discern what is the will of God, what is good and acceptable and perfect."
Romans 12:2 ESV

ENGAGING, ENCOURAGING CULTURE

Gaining the value of combined intelligence by igniting the fire of passion

"Developing a constructive culture, one in which all team members are respected and the organizational values are embraced, is a leadership imperative. It cannot be delegated or ignored!"

A star professional football player made headlines by striking his future wife – knocking her unconscious – in a public place. The reason that this violence was remarkable had less to do with the rarity of such abuse, but that it was captured on a security camera. The media played and replayed the video while delving into other examples of domestic violence within the professional football community. While the pundits questioned whether football encouraged a culture of violence, the National Football League was slow to respond. Their public statements and sanctions lacked both clarity and conviction, implying that the events were isolated and not directly relevant to the culture of the sport. Only in the following weeks did the league begin to take a strong stand and acknowledge its initial lack of leadership in establishing a positive culture.

All organizations have a culture – the collective set of values and beliefs that provide the framework for how we treat each other and what we accomplish. Too often, however, there is little focus on that culture – on evaluating whether it is actively supporting our purpose or impeding it. It is even less common that deliberate steps are taken to change the culture.

"Change values?" you may ask. "How can you challenge people's personal beliefs in this age of political correctness?"

Excellent question. Yet, there is an answer. We address culture by addressing its "artifacts", the behaviors. In that way we do not need to delve into philosophical discussions of values or motivations. There is no need to debate the validity of beliefs or what happened in the past. Instead, we discuss, model and encourage behaviors that meet the agreed norms. Our first step is to help the organization define the desired culture in terms of engagement and behaviors. The question is, "How do we expect to interact and how can we encourage each individual to embrace these behaviors?"

> *"By developing a positive, encouraging culture we create an environment where leaders emerge, energy abounds and success flourishes!"*

Let's start with those that we have already discussed; namely, our purpose, processes, teamwork and commitment. We all seek to accomplish something of value and to do it efficiently as a team. Those are attributes of a healthy culture – one that nearly all team members will embrace. Earlier chapters explored the roles of leaders in developing these key concepts and the importance of involving a broad spectrum of the team in that process. This is a first step in developing the desired culture.

Next, it is helpful to pursue two additional aspects of culture:

First is the degree to which individuals are committed to the organization's purpose. The second is how we interact with one another in terms of observable behaviors.

There are many ways to measure the engagement of team members – a prime indicator of their commitment. One of the most researched and accepted methods is the Gallup® Consulting Employee Engagement survey[12]. This survey determines the distribution of individuals that are engaged, not engaged and actively disengaged. According to Gallup, top performing organizations typically have about two thirds of the employees engaged and less than ten percent actively disengaged.

We build on the Gallup® approach by adding the *pervasive leadership* model. In our model we consider the following reference points on the commitment continuum:

- Pervasive leaders – those that are highly engaged and seeking to influence others. These are the "interveners" who actively seek to establish expectations, reach out to others, anticipate needs and solve problems. These are the team members who see their role as more than implementers, but as owners who seek to improve the process and increase the engagement of

---

[12] Gallup Consulting® Employee Engagement – How to Improve Employee Engagement in the Workplace - Gallup

others.

- Engaged implementers – those that are focused on outcomes and personally committed to achieving the organizational goals. These are the "active implementers" who are eager to support the organizational goals.

- Non-engaged implementers – those who work to externally defined expectations but feel little personal connection to the outcome. These are the "passive implementers" who prefer comfort to accomplishment or are fearful of failure.

- Inhibitors – those who are actively disengaged, finding barriers to achieving their assigned roles and often drawing energy and focus away from the core work.

The goal in this model, like that of Gallup®, is to move people up the commitment continuum. Not all people will pick up the leadership mantel, but dramatic improvement occurs when 20-25% do. They form the catalyst to move others from the "non-engaged" to "engaged" category gaining the energy, insights and ability of the majority and making it less comfortable to be an "inhibitor".

We do not link these roles to positions in the organizational structure. You can have people with senior leadership titles who are disengaged. While the expectation is organizational managers are truly leaders, the power of *pervasive leadership* is that it permeates the organization – making the organizational chart more about function than influence on others. For example, a manager is responsible for budgets, reporting, etc. but may not be effective at inspiring others.

What are the characteristics of people who can build this energizing culture? Here is a concise summary of those attributes that, when encouraged, play a vital role in in establishing the desired culture

Leaders who develop positive cultures demonstrate:

- Self-confidence: They are not timid or arrogant, but through life experiences face obstacles and create solutions.

- Empathy: They value others' thoughts feelings and are led to act with compassion when things are not right.

- Self-Control: They control their attention, thoughts, emotions and actions allowing them to focus on what is important.

- Integrity: They are consistent in demonstrating honesty and fulfilling their commitments to others and the organization.

- Curiosity: They are not afraid to ask, "what if?" and consider other points of view.

- Perseverance: They recognize that success requires overcoming obstacles and adaptability.

These attributes are not based on a person's position on the organization. Their true value is demonstrated when we identify them throughout the organization and enlist them in the plan to develop a constructive culture.

It should be noted that this list was adapted from an unlikely source[13] demonstrating the value of looking beyond the traditional approaches to challenging problems.

One specific responsibility that organizational leaders cannot delegate is addressing the *inhibitors*. There are many constructive ways of achieving this; clarifying roles and expectations or finding another position that better matches their skills and interests, to name a couple. We will provide another constructive approach to address *inhibitors* later in this chapter. The important point is that inhibitors are not allowed to continue in that role – this is a major challenge in developing *pervasive leadership*.

The second aspect of culture is the organization's behavioral norms. These are the accepted ways that we interact with others and approach our assignments. We have discussed clarity of purpose, the value of processes, strong teamwork, commitment and innovation. In growing organizations, these are underlying values directly supported by constructive behaviors. Note how these are reflected in another following Gallup® summary:

Gallup - Key Characteristics of Engaged Cultures[14]

---

[13] Adapted from: 7 Skills Separate Successful Kids from Those Who Struggle" by Michele Borba These 7 skills separate successful kids from 'those who struggle': Psychologist and parenting expert (cnbc.com)

- **Warm Relationships** – *friendly colleagues*
  - **Honesty** – *open, humble interactions*
    - **Shared Accountability and Performance**
      - **Alignment on Shared Goals**

While these examples are clear and compelling, they do not address how we create a stronger culture as defined by broad acceptance of these concepts in words and actions.

In most cases, the organizational culture is neutral or positive but not well defined. In these cases, a fairly low-key approach often works to bring more focus and support on building positive relationships among individuals and groups.

> *"Mutual Respect and Trust are the foundation of a Constructive Culture."*

The most basic elements of a positive culture are mutual **respect** and **trust**. We show respect by the way we interact with each other. Speaking to each other respectfully and actively listening to understand others' viewpoints are essential. Openness and actively involving others in decisions are key elements in building trust.

Our actions must be consistent with our words and professed values. When leaders throughout the organization apply these basic principles and support others in their application, positive change will flourish.

---

[14] What Engaged Employees Say About Your Brand (gallup.com)

We applied this low-key approach in a large organization where there was a lack of respect and trust between management and bargaining unit representatives. We started by jointly agreeing simple ground rules: actively listening, using questions instead of judgmental statements, seeking common understanding, eliminating cursing and openly discussing the basis for decisions.

> *"Words translated into observable behaviors provided the basis for establishing the desired culture."*

We established a "word picture" of our desired interrelationships, not unlike the Gallup model summarized above. We held each other accountable for acting consistent with the desired behaviors. Most important was following through on promises – an expression of honesty and respect.

While it was not immediate, this simple approach was a major step in building respect and trust in the organization. With this foundation, morale, commitment and performance all improved.

After seeing success in our limited approach, we decided to take a more systematic approach to developing a positive culture. This simple approach included the following steps:

- Developing a broad list of observable behaviors associated with constructive cultures. Where possible, several words with similar meanings were used to provide a broader, more understandable picture of the desired behaviors.

   A broad range of first-line supervisors and supportive team members developed the initial list of behaviors. In hindsight, the peoples selected for this activity exhibited the attributes summarized a few pages earlier.

The resulting list is provided in the following table.

A Constructive Culture Defined by Behaviors

Key Behavior	Similar Behaviors
Accepting	Friendly, Welcoming
Active	Dynamic, Energized
Aligned	United, Consistent
Authentic	Sincere, Open
Caring	Friendly, Compassionate
Collaborative	Involved, Engaged
Efficient	Effective, Intuitive
Empowered	Authorized, Responsible
Encouraging	Inviting, Uplifting
Energizing	Compelling, Inspiring
Honest	Integrity, Truthful, Open
Innovative	Creative, Adaptable
Organized	Coordinated, Prepared
Questioning	Evaluating, Probing
Respectful	Valuing, Listening
Successful	Achieving, Productive
Supportive	Connected, Helpful
Systematic	Organized, Planned
Supportive	Encouraging, Empathetic

- Once the basic behaviors were identified we used a simple survey to assess where we were as an overall organization and withing the sub-groups. The survey asks two questions concerning each Key Behavior:

    a. How important is this behavior in achieving our goals?

    b. To what extent do we currently demonstrate this behavior?

    In addition, "write-in" statements were encouraged to provide additional insights. A broad sampling of the organization was surveyed to capture the results at a team level while assuring that the results are not linked to individuals.

- The teams analyzed the survey results. Both organization wide results and those for each work group were evaluated. The purpose was twofold; first, to identify behaviors that were considered especially important where there was already a high degree of performance. Secondly, to identify those few, core behaviors that were considered essential to a healthy work environment and those where there was the biggest gap between the desired and current demonstration of those behaviors. Once developed, these data were summarized in a way that provided a clear, compelling picture of the desired culture and behaviors.

The survey results were shared in small group meetings to validate the conclusions and provide insights on how they could be used to improve our relationships. Emphasis was placed on highlighting the strong areas and asking how they could be leveraged to improve the culture in the areas of low performance.

In some cases, people were critical of the effort suspecting that it was just another program that would soon fade away. The difference, however, was that their peers engaged in the discussions and appeared to believe that the approach would work. Another, soon to be revealed difference was that formal leaders began to hold themselves accountable to the same behaviors.

The process did not end with these meetings where ideas were exchanged and we looked into our team members' eyes and asked for their commitment to implement the approach.

Following those initial meetings, we continued to clarify and reinforce these values. People throughout the organization were engaged in all phases of the process emphasizing the concept of *pervasive leadership*. Additional actions included:

- Once these few important characteristics were identified, they were explained in a compelling behavioral context. Some were organization wide, others focused on specific sub-groups. Examples included:
    - We are respectful of one another – investing in our relationships by seeking understanding and establishing common goals.

    - We are collaborative - involving the team in key decisions and valuing their contributions in strengthening our performance.

- We focus on success – both in the accomplishment and the process and relationships used to accomplish it.

- Integrating the cultural picture into all aspects of the organization. For example, when a group achieved a notable success, we invested time in understanding the cultural and teamwork aspects that contributed to that success. Likewise, when we missed a significant goal, we encouraged discussion of the cultural and teamwork issues that contributed to that failure. It was important to focus on these as learning activities involving a wide range of team members. The goal was learning, not identifying those at fault.

- In some cases, specific actions were taken to develop the desired behaviors where significant gaps were identified; however, the use of "campaigns" was minimized. Developing the desired behaviors and drawing them into the culture is a process not an event. It's through integration, building them into our daily routine and discussions that they become real.

- Leadership accountability to the behavioral standards was emphasized. It was not initially easy for leaders, particularly those with leadership titles to acknowledge their personal shortcomings, but when we started doing that, it was well-received, particularly when that confession included an openness for feedback from others.

It was important to emphasize the outcome in terms of relationships, not just high-sounding phrases to hang on the walls. Our purpose was to define who we are in terms of our relationships and behaviors. It was to establish expectations and integrate them into our daily conversations and, more important, our actions.

The results were amazing. After a year there was appropriate pride within individuals and workgroups. Individuals were acknowledging the importance of relationships with other groups. Most striking was the change from bouncing problems up to "management" for resolution to reaching out to other individuals or organizations to collaborate on resolving issues.

> *"Clarity on the prerequisites for success is another critical cultural attribute that can be developed."*

A different approach was used in another organization – one that had a generally positive culture but lacked clarity on why we were not being as successful as others in our same industry.

In this case, we focused on the concepts of this book utilizing the *Seven Characteristics of Successful Organizations* as a framework. We systematically created understanding and commitment within workgroups and focused on how each group supported the broader organizational goals.

The concept of *pervasive leadership* was developed with application to specific roles and activities. We methodically developed leadership skills using the approaches discussed previously. We used temporary assignments of individuals to work in other areas both to gain insights and to help the other organization see and resolve inefficiencies in their processes.

As a part of this effort, we developed the following summary of attributes for success and encouraged their use both by individuals and organizationally. The concepts of fulfilling **Career Aspirations**, discussed in the next chapter, contributed to this success.

Seven Attributes of Successful People[15]

Pursue Your Passion	*Fulfill those aspirations that energize you.*
Know Yourself & Others	*Understand and leverage your personality and understanding of others.*
Develop a Growth Mindset	*Seek to grow your personal and the organization's value.*
Embrace Opportunity	*Take initiative in seeking new experiences.*
Develop Purposeful Relationships	*Share passions, experience and knowledge.*

---

[15] Adapted from "***Career Aspirations – Finding True Success in your Career***" by Bryce Shriver, et. al. Available at Amazon.com

Manage Your Lifestyle	*Assure that lifestyle does not limit your career.*
Focus on What is Important	*Honor relationships and core values*

> *"While the focus is on establishing the desired culture, there are some values and behaviors that must be eliminated."*

There are also a few values and behaviors that we must discourage – those that must be overtly addressed through leadership and constructive peer pressure. The most prominent of these include disrespect for others, arrogance and anger. In each case, individuals or groups expressing these behaviors are placing their personal interests above those of the broader team. Additional examples of unacceptable behaviors are dishonesty, cynicism and apathy.

Again, it is through gaining support for positive, constructive behaviors that the *pervasive leadership* approach can help identify and address these unwelcome behaviors before they adversely affect the organization.

While establishing a positive, performance-oriented culture is important, it is not easy. In cases where there is not a healthy culture, a more rigorous process may be required.

In one company there was a deep rift between management and the skilled workers who were essential to its success following a union contract dispute. The interface between work groups was also stressed due to differing views on how the contract dispute was resolved. In this case, we decided that professional help was needed to rebuild trust and build a foundation to create a constructive culture. This process worked well but required extensive leadership involvement and support from an external consulting company.

A company that has a comprehensive approach for building a constructive culture is Human Synergistics International[16]. They include a complete suite of products built around twelve behaviors. Their statistically validated process included methods for defining the existing organizational culture and related leadership behaviors. Their approach coupled with strong leadership allowed us to address the underlying cultural challenges that stifled our success.

Summary

The success of any organization relies on a positive, success-oriented culture. At its heart, an organization's culture is defined by relationships – how people and work groups interact with each other. A positive culture is built on **Respect** and **Trust**.

There are many approaches that may be applied to building an energizing, aligned culture. One mistake that many organizations make is not addressing a negative, underlying culture.

---

[16] Human Synergistics International® – Organizational Culture Change & Leadership | Human Synergistics

As noted in the opening of this chapter, there are times that the organization's culture stresses its very fabric. Leaders who recognize these challenges and commit to making a positive change in culture will be successful. While senior leaders must set high expectations, the truth comes through *pervasive leadership* in clarifying the desired relationships through clarity of words, examples and rewards.

Application: Engaging Encouraging Culture

1. Research different methods for defining a positive, encouraging culture such as those discussed in this chapter. Use this information to refine the list of desired team behaviors summarized above.

2. Conduct a simple survey with team members and members of interfacing teams to define the desired behavior-based culture. Collaborate with the team to define how the desired culture will be developed.

3. Develop a constructive relationship with an individual who will provide valid, candid feedback to you both when your personal behaviors meet the desired standards and when they are not consistent with the expectations.

"But the fruit of the Spirit is love, joy, peace, patience, kindness, goodness, faithfulness, gentleness, self-control; against such things there is no law."
Galatians 5:22-23. ESV

PERVASIVE LEADERSHIP

Expanding the circle of success by multiplying true leaders

"True leadership is not inherited; it is not an entitlement nor is it bestowed due to position. It is earned through an active commitment to the purpose, values and people of the organization. It is demonstrated by the courage to advocate and do the right thing, even when not expedient."

Pervasive leadership! This concept is expressed by leadership being distributed throughout the organization, not based on a hierarchy as in the classic military model. We have explored the importance of engaging leaders throughout the organization in defining the organization's purpose, building teamwork, demonstrating commitment, encouraging innovation and developing a collaborative culture.

What is there to add? The next step is to intentionally develop *pervasive leadership* instead of relying on those with leadership titles to fulfill those roles. Let's start by summarizing the implications of positional and *pervasive leadership*.

Purpose: While a board of directors or executives may define the overall purpose of an organization, it is only empowering when the purpose is personal to individuals and work groups throughout the organization. It's only when they understand both the broader purpose and their unique role in achieving those goals that the publicized purpose takes life. When leaders at all levels link individual and team contributions to achieving a worthwhile goal, the organization's goal becomes a reality.

Process: While many organizations hire experts to design a process or continue to use those developed a decade ago based on the then current technology, they will never achieve their full potential. It's only when individuals throughout the organization, particularly those closest to the work, take ownership of the process that it becomes more intuitive, effective and efficient. Again, this requires leaders, whatever their official title, to assess the existing processes, identify the weak links and enact changes to improve the quality and cost of the product or service. "Not my job," some may say. This means that *pervasive leadership* is not yet rooted in the culture.

Teamwork: Processes only work when the skills, both technical and interpersonal, of the individuals match those required for success. With traditional, top-down leadership, there is often insufficient focus on this critical aspect. Instead, there may be over-dependence on traditional position descriptions. When *pervasive leadership* exists, there is a stronger ability to match team skills through a combination of process changes, developing the skills within the work group and realigning individuals' roles to match their strengths to the workflow. This is often developed by collaboration among those on the team that is encouraged by organic leaders.

Commitment: One key attribute of true leaders is a commitment and a passion for success. In the traditional organization, the positional leader is responsible for cheering the group toward the goal. When leadership is distributed throughout the organization, ownership for accomplishing the organization's goals becomes intrinsic. Pervasive leaders take a stand when things are not going well, seeking to correct and address the underlying issues instead of waiting for "management" to respond.

Innovation: Traditional, hierarchical organizations are slow to change, innovate or adapt since change requires layers of justification and approval. Pervasive leadership encourages those closest to the work to seek better methods, faster technology and stronger interfaces. Where individuals and groups have the authority to make changes, improvement flourishes. Of course, ground rules must be established, but with the philosophy of reaching across traditional organizational boundaries to achieve better results, change tends to be better thought out, more widely accepted and more beneficial.

Culture: The culture is a summation of the accepted behavioral norms of the organization. Establishing a constructive culture is a key leadership responsibility, perhaps second only to defining the organization's purpose. In the traditional organization, the positional leader is charged with defining and encouraging the desired culture. With *pervasive leadership*, the clarification and reinforcement of constructive behavioral norms is ever-present. There is less opportunity for a negative sub-culture to take root. Instead, a commitment to the overall organization's goals is paramount. *Pervasive leadership* is encouraging, always intervening and focuses on building a collaborative team motivated by achievement.

"If pervasive leadership is so great, why isn't it pervasive in modern organizations?"

"This is a question that true leaders both ask and address!"

Leadership: We return to the fundamental question. If *pervasive leadership* is so great, why isn't it pervasive in today's organizations? The answer is fairly simple – to encourage *pervasive leadership* requires that the hierarchical leaders give up some control – to accept that the people within the organization understand the goals and values of the organization and will faithfully work within that framework. It requires them to change their paradigm, moving out of their comfort zone. This requires either a brave manager or agreement within the traditional management structure to accept the new model wholeheartedly. Both are uncommon.

So, with that in mind, how do we start?

First, we start by identifying those with the aptitude and desire to play a leadership role even if they do not have that title. Typically, it is easy to identify these individuals. They are the ones that get things done. They accomplish their roles without fanfare. They reach out to others to help them achieve their goals, they take the lead in resolving problems and demonstrate a positive attitude.

These leaders have strong character, competence and commitment. These attributes are the foundation of leadership as defined in the following table. They are collaborative and demonstrate an aptitude for success.

LEADERSHIP

Character	Competence	Commitment
Integrity: ✓ Loyal ✓ Honest ✓ Authentic ✓ Courageous **Intent:** ✓ Caring ✓ Inclusive ✓ Encouraging	**Capability:** ✓ Skill ✓ Knowledge ✓ Experience ✓ Judgement **Performance:** ✓ Consistent ✓ Reliable ✓ Results	**Present:** ✓ Active ✓ Engaged ✓ Understand ✓ Constructive **Inspiring:** ✓ Strategic ✓ Energizing ✓ Passionate

These criteria are useful in identifying potential leaders. The next step is encouraging them to assume a leadership role. The goal is to develop their individual leadership skills by granting both the freedom and authority to make improvements.

Start by collaborating with them to identify an area for improvement that they cannot accomplish alone. Likely candidates include process improvements, evaluation of new technology, developing a stronger personnel safety infrastructure or establishing key performance measures. No, planning the annual Christmas party or Independence Day celebration does not count!

Once the application is identified, preferably with active involvement of the work groups, the purpose, goals, budgets, constraints and feedback process should be clarified. The overall purpose of broadening individual involvement and leadership should be clearly established.

The supporting, traditional leader must then move into the coaching role with a primary focus on supporting the team by providing the resources needed for them to be successful. The key attributes, purpose, process, teamwork, commitment, culture, innovation and leadership should be integrated into the plan. They must be discussed and modeled as a key element of the transition to *pervasive leadership*. The group must be set free to pursue their purpose, apply their leadership and address their challenges.

The end goal is to empower all employees through a deep understanding and acceptance of their roles and responsibilities. It's about commitment to establishing a culture of success, of individual courage and passion for achievement. It's demonstrated when individuals at all levels seek to do the right thing instead of the previously accepted approach which resulted in mediocrity in both performance and spirit.

Pervasive leadership provides great value, yet there is risk. If all are accountable for results, is any one truly accountable? There will always be a role for the traditional, hierarchical leader. Organizations define certain responsibilities to individuals in certain positions. This is necessary and desirable – it provides order, it streamlines decisions, and it provides clarity and security. What are these unique roles of the traditional, hierarchical leader that relies on positional authority?

Examples include:

- Providing clarity of purpose and priorities by helping the team see what is important now in terms of the longer-term goals.

- Defining organizational imperatives and constraints, such as, regulatory compliance, financial controls, budgets, staffing levels, etc.

- Establishing the framework for a constructive culture through actions and, when necessary, words.

- Developing leadership skills in others - giving them opportunity and accepting failures as a normal part of the learning process.

- Clarifying the organization's values, directly linking them to roles and responsibilities.

- Providing needed resources and breaking down barriers that impede organizational effectiveness.

- Disciplining team members in those few cases where they refuse to meet performance or conduct standards.

- Accepting responsibility for group failures, for understanding the underlying causes and implementing corrective actions.

- Assertively addressing events or issues that are not consistent with the organization's goals or culture.

- Communicating in times of crises – being the focal point for internal and external stakeholders.

"What if I am passionate about improving performance and desire to help lead the needed change?

Must I just wait to be discovered?"

Perhaps, you do not hold a leadership title but are passionate about improving the group's performance. Must you wait to be discovered by the titled leaders? How do you get noticed without appearing to be self-serving?

Start by developing and demonstrating the leadership attributes summarized in the table above. Second, look for opportunities to collaborate with others to identify and implement process improvements. The following table provides a good summary of attitudes that will provide the needed opportunities.

Creating Pervasive Leaders[17]

True leaders – those that lead change to accomplish more:

1. Don't wait for a title to lead – exercising influence is not limited by position.
2. Are graciously disruptive – asking "What if?" and "Why not?"
3. Think for themselves and are not limited by the current paradigm.

---

[17] Adapted from "11 Surprising Habits of Powerful People" by Travis Bradbury

4. Focus on what truly matters – those few things that lead to improvement.
5. Master conflict by directly and constructively drawing people together.
6. Inspire conversation – asking questions to gain insight and understanding.
7. Know their strengths and weaknesses – seeking those who complement their skills.
8. Grow and leverage their networks – adding, as well as receiving, value.
9. Ask for help – encourage honest feedback on direction, approaches and decisions.
10. Believe that the "dream" is possible by being optimistic, energetic and passionate.
11. Do it NOW – not waiting until all details are aligned and all risk eliminated.

Our book, *Career Aspirations – Finding True Success in Your Career*, may be helpful in developing these skills.

"Pervasive Leadership is required for success in the 21st century. The need for true leadership has never been greater. A new generation of leaders is eager to lead. Will we embrace these opportunities? That is the remaining question."

As we close this chapter it is important to accept that not all people want to be leaders – many people are happier to work hard within defined roles. That is fine, there is a need for people who do real work to high standards. We should welcome them but encourage them to support their peers who do want to lead. What we cannot accept are those who "lead" against us either actively or passively.

This book started with a passionate description of "what leaders do". It provided a general vision. The rest of the book has explained how an organization's power comes from within – from *pervasive leadership*. That is our quest, it is where we will find success and fulfillment.

Let's close with one additional example. During one of the organizational crises discussed earlier in the book, two bargaining unit employees suggested that we pursue gaining "STAR" status under the U.S. Occupational Safety and Health Administration's Voluntary Protection Program[18] (VPP). This OSHA program is unique in recognizing three aspects of safety; high industrial safety performance, robust safety programs and a strong commitment to safety expressed throughout the organization. If all three are present, OSHA recognizes the organization with its highest-level STAR recognition.

---

[18] Voluntary Protection Programs | Occupational Safety and Health Administration (osha.gov)

At the time, we were immersed in change with many improvement plans and priorities. The organization and leadership were stressed by the magnitude and urgency of the changes. Our industrial safety performance was acceptable – actually one of our better areas. I was inclined to turn down the employees' offer citing the existing priorities and workload. The employees sensed my lack of enthusiasm but instead of accepting it, continued to explain the benefits, which included an opportunity for management and bargaining unit employees to work together to achieve a goal we all supported.

I asked what they needed of me and the senior leadership team.

"Only your verbal support giving us the time to meet the program administrative requirements," they responded. "We will do the work."

How could I refuse? Yet, it was hard for me to get out of their way and let them achieve this important goal. Reluctantly, I agreed and watched as they accomplished that goal. We became one of the first organizations in our industry to achieve OSHA's STAR status. It was a bit humbling to admit that I nearly killed this important step in the organization's development but, in the end, it was an important step in my understanding of *pervasive leadership* – one of many!

Summary

Success requires that individuals throughout the organization accept ownership for achieving its goals. This is the essence of *pervasive leadership* and is developed through a systematic application of the *Seven Characteristics of Effective Organizations* that provide the outline for this book. True leaders embrace these concepts and engage others in their application.

There are two interrelated prerequisites for developing *pervasive leadership*; namely, a commitment by titled leaders and a desire by those withing the organization to implement this transformational organizational change.

The rewards far outweigh the cost. The time to start is now!

Application: Pervasive Leadership

1. Develop a list of leadership roles in your organization. Which ones are traditional, hierarchical roles and which can be distributed? Ask others on your team and interfacing teams to challenge the list since it is often hard to shift our traditional view of leadership roles.

2. Conduct a simple workshop on *pervasive leadership* concepts and the list developed in application 1 above. Seek agreement within the team on applications of this concept in strengthening team performance.

3. Develop a personal list of areas where you can release some control to strengthen team commitment and develop leadership skills in other team members. Implement that plan.

4. Consider using the 11 Behaviors outlined in the table "**Creating Pervasive Leaders**" provided in this chapter. You may be amazed at the impact that you will have.

"Where there is no guidance (leadership) the people fall (fail); but in a multitude of counselors (leaders) there is safety (success)."
Proverbs 11:14 NKJV (modified)

CLOSING – OR IS IT THE BEGINNING?

*The quest for success never ends –
it is an ever-continuing journey*

"Our quest is not about compensation, recognition or promotions. Our journey is about making a difference – about creating the future, enjoying life and knowing that our organization and society are better because we are committed to success."

As we bring this short essay to a close, we must ask "what next?" Do we file this, along with the other reference books that have preceded it? Or do we choose to apply its insights – to accept a new paradigm that defines leadership in terms of roles instead of titles?

We have not focused on organizational charts or hierarchy. We have not discussed "fairness" or "opportunity". We have focused on developing *pervasive leadership* as the key to success. Opportunity abounds – it's our role as leaders to seize it. In the *pervasive leadership* model, there is plenty of opportunity for each of us to be successful.

Will we be the change that is so clearly needed?

What will you do today? Will you take the first steps toward building a *pervasive leadership* team? Will you choose to become the leader that you, and others, desire to follow?

The first step in this quest is to develop an understanding of true success and the personal attributes that lead to this success. Next, we seek to develop our leadership skills while not waiting to be recognized with a leadership title. These form a foundation for pursuing *pervasive leadership* throughout the organization. Our goal is to create an effective team – an environment where we focus our talents and efforts on achieving a common purpose.

In summary, let's pursue that goal by exploring four concepts; namely:

- Clearly defining success in personal terms – not in salary but in deep, inner satisfaction.

- Developing the attributes of successful people.

- Enhancing our personal leadership skills.

- Pursuing *Pervasive Leadership* in our organization

We will explore each in turn.

Defining Success

We may fall into the trap of defining success in material terms; salary, position, power, etc. Yet, at the end of our career there will be other, more meaningful, measures of success that we will cherish.

These include:

- ✓ Finding "our place" on the team – that place where we use our unique skills and personality to achieve a worthy goal.

- ✓ Growing personally by developing understanding, wisdom and compassion.

- ✓ Creating a better product, process, or service to benefit society.

- ✓ Encouraging others to seek the fullness of their potential.

- ✓ Standing firm when encouraged to compromise our integrity or core values.

- ✓ Providing strength and stability in times of crisis.

- ✓ Building our legacy by developing people, processes and products that will have value after we retire.

- ✓ Having an energizing respect for the organization we serve and those who lead it.

- ✓ Fulfilling our sense of purpose and accomplishment driven by a deep, inner passion, to accomplish goals bigger than a single individual can achieve.

- ✓ Holding a positive view of the future – an encouraging expectation of personal development, opportunity and rewards.

✓ Sleeping well at night, in peace, knowing that what we accomplished is of value and that we did it with integrity.

These are the true measures of success - accomplishments of lasting value, the ideals that we pass down to the next generation whether it be our organization or our children.

Developing the Attributes of Successful People

Our research suggests that successful people share several attributes. The following table provides seven of these attributes which can be developed. Our book, ***Career Aspirations – Finding True Success in Your Career***", explains each attribute and provides insights in how to develop each in terms of our personal definition of success.

Seven Attributes of Successful People[19]

Pursue Your Passion	*Fulfill those aspirations that energize you*
Know Yourself & Others	*Understand and leverage your personality and understanding of others*
Develop a Growth Mindset	*Seek to grow your personal and the organization's value*

---

[19] From "*Career Aspirations – Finding True Success in your Career*" by Bryce Shriver, et. al. ©2022 by Three Seven Research, Inc. Available at Amazon.com

Embrace Opportunity	*Take initiative in seeking new experiences*
Develop Purposeful Relationships	*Share passions, experience and knowledge*
Manage Your Lifestyle	*Assure that lifestyle does not limit your career*
Focus on What is Important	*Honor relationships and core values*

Do you exhibit each of these characteristics? What are your strengths? Where is additional effort warranted?

Enhancing Our Leadership Skills

We begin by developing our own leadership skills, by becoming the leader that we want to replicate throughout the organization. We do this by understanding our own strengths and weaknesses by actively seeking input from others as we seek to help them.

> *"Once we understand success and the attributes that lead to it, It is time to pursue it with vigor by developing our leadership skills and then leading others to pervasive leadership."*

What about tangible steps? Reading and applying the principles of this book is a great first step – you are already farther along than the majority of people who only perused the cover.

Here are some more specific suggestions:

- Highlight the roles of leaders in the *Leadership Crisis* chapter. Highlight those that you have a good grasp of and those warranting future development. Pursue developing and applying them in your current role.

- Understand yourself by using any number of personality profiles – Myers Briggs Type Indicator, Birkman, and Organizational Cultural Inventory. There are many available at no cost through a simple web search. The key objective is to learn how to leverage your temperament to become more influential within the organization.

- Evaluate your current leadership approach by comparing your traits to the **Seven Attributes of Successful People** (above) and **Traits of Successful Leaders** provided below. What are your strengths? What areas are worthy of additional development?

- Assess the degree that your current organization exhibits the *Seven Characteristic of Successful Organizations* described in earlier chapters of this book. Highlight strengths and clarify any gaps in meeting the aspirations.

- Understand and help shape the cultural leadership norms of your organization. Where does your style match that expected by the organization and where are there gaps? Where is there a need to change the norm?

- Gather a group of your peers to look at one aspect of a key process to identify the specific areas where it can be improved to achieve the desired outcome faster, cheaper and with better quality.

- Identify a peer who you respect and ask them to observe you and provide candid feedback both in areas where you excel and those where you can improve. Always thank them for the feedback, even when it hurts or seems unfounded – it is a gift.

Common Traits of Successful Leaders[20]

1. Intelligence – Continuous Learning
2. Building Strong Relationships with Influencers
3. Warrior Worth Ethic
4. Laser Focus
5. Productive Habits
6. Visibility
7. Positive Mental Outlook
8. Anticipation
9. Clear Vision
10. Persistence
11. Courageous

---

[20] https://richhabits.net/leadership-series-common-traits-of-successful-leaders-trait-1-intelligence/

12. Master the Fundamentals
13. Effective Communicators
14. Outlier Mindset

Pursuing Pervasive Leadership

Once you assume a leadership role, developing a *pervasive leadership* team involves two major components; the ability to ask insightful, provocative questions and the courage to take a stand in building a constructive culture. Remember, you can pursue this quest even if your title does not reflect that role.

> *"Developing pervasive leadership is not easy. First, It demands that we exhibit the attributes of success. It also demands that we have the courage to release control – that we ask questions instead of directing others to meet our desires."*

What is the purpose of asking provocative questions, particularly when we know the answer? Why not just share our wisdom or, if it appears to be more constructive, we can just formulate our statement as a question?

Our purpose is to gain support, to build a deep, intrinsic understanding of our purpose and how we want to accomplish it. We do it to model the constructive culture and develop leaders throughout the organization.

If our goal is to develop rather than direct, what types of questions do we ask? In addition, when do we ask questions rather than just do the work?

Let's address the second question first – when do we ask questions? The answer is straight forward – we ask them when there is a need for direction. If the process is flowing smoothly, and the team is working well – let it flow, do the work. If, however, there is a bottleneck, a disruption in the flow, it is time for leadership to help the team identify and correct the underlying issues.

In the classic leadership model, the process may come to a halt waiting for "management" to address the issue. In the *pervasive leadership* model, individuals within the group collaborate to seek resolution. In most cases it involves asking questions and then working together to find answers. What type of questions?

- What is our goal? What are we trying to achieve?

- How should this work? What are the key steps or elements that must be accomplished to achieve the desired outcome?

- How can we define the challenge, not in terms of who made a mistake, but in terms of what actually happened vs. what was desired and expected?

- Is our problem a result of not implementing the plan as intended or is the process itself weak, not accounting for all important steps or attributes?

- What were the causes – not just the direct cause, but those hidden contributors that were lurking below the surface?

- Who else should we involve in the solution – what additional skill or experience do we need?

- What could I do to avoid or resolve this problem? What can we do collectively?

- How can we improve our effectiveness? How can we make our job more rewarding?

- What can we learn and apply to the future?

The purpose is to properly focus on the challenge – to constructively seek to define the issue, its underlying causes and, most importantly, solutions. It is to draw others into the discussion and resolution. In doing so, we gain understanding and commitment. We help develop a constructive culture and build the picture of success. We encourage leadership in others by seeking their insights and respecting their views.

Lastly, there is the question of courage. We often think of the battlefield hero who risks his life to save another. Yes, that is true courage, but so is moving out of our comfort zone to build a stronger, more effective organization. It takes courage to:

✓ Understand my role and take joy in doing it well by understanding how it fits into our team's overall purpose.

✓ Challenge the status quo when we see a better way.

✓ Focus on solving problems rather than assigning blame.

- ✓ Encourage someone who is struggling – offering tangible support.

- ✓ Embrace other views and feedback concerning our personal performance.

- ✓ Develop new skills and adopt new approaches to enhance the team's performance.

- ✓ Maintain your team values while not being closed to different views.

- ✓ Welcome the idea that your paradigm is incorrect or incomplete and encourage development and implementation of a better approach.

Developing *pervasive leadership* is not easy. I trust that you will accept the challenge. I did and found life much richer as a result - even as I continue that quest in this journey, we call life.

Application: Closing – or is it the Beginning

1. Reflect on a recent team success. What made it successful? How were the *Seven Characteristics of Successful Organizations* manifested?

2. Review the notes you developed over the course of this book. What are your three most significant leadership strengths? What are the two areas that warrant additional development?

3. Define one leadership attribute that you want to master. Develop a true plan for achieving your goal including specific actions, schedules and accountability for mastering this skill.

"Finally, brothers, whatever is true, whatever is honorable, whatever is just, whatever is pure, whatever is lovely, whatever is commendable, if there is any excellence, if there is anything worthy of praise, think about these things."
Philippians 4:8 ESV

Three Seven Research

© Three Seven Research, Inc. 2022

THREE-SEVEN RESEARCH

Developing leaders by applying 21st Century Innovation with the Timeless Principles of the 1st Century.

Three-Seven Research's purpose is to improve organizational effectiveness and personal growth by developing true leaders. The underlying concepts are based on over three decades of research and application of innovative approaches to identify and develop leadership principles that can be applied to build a better future for all.

The name, Three-Seven Research, comes from the three essential functions of true leaders and the seven core principles of successful organizations.

Wise leaders build their organization,
They establish the seven pillars of a successful organization.
Adapted from Proverbs 9:1

The *Three Essential Leadership* functions are:

- Define the organization's purpose and vision of success.
- Develop the organization, processes and culture needed to achieve that vision.
- Assure that the vision is actually achieved.

Our research has identified *Seven Characteristics of Successful Organizations*:

- <u>Clarity of Purpose</u> – a clear and compelling reason for its existence.
- <u>Intuitive, Effective Processes</u> – applying the unique talents of individuals with technology to provide consistent, excellent results.
- <u>Exceptional Teamwork</u> – developing attitudes and skills needed to multiply individual contributions.
- <u>Commitment to Organizational Success</u> – seeing the organization's purpose as more important than individual goals.
- <u>Innovation and Renewal</u> – willingness to try new ideas and approaches.
- <u>Energizing Culture</u> – encouraging, respectful and solution oriented.
- <u>Enlightened and Pervasive Leadership</u> – leaders throughout the organization encouraging each of the other characteristics.

"Wisdom has built her house; she has hewn out her seven pillars."
Proverbs 9:1 NKJV

The name also refers to our spiritual heritage where three represents the Holy Trinity and seven is God's number of completeness.

Meet the Authors

Collectively, the authors have over 40 years of leadership experience with each contributing to the areas of technology, process improvement and leadership. They represent three generations with experience in the military, education, public utilities, communications, finance and manufacturing. Each has focused on personal development with the purpose of improving their personal skills and the effectiveness of their organization.

Bryce L. Shriver, Ph.D., MBA, M.S., B.S.

> Bryce Shriver enjoyed a 40-year career in the power industry beginning as an engineer in the U.S. Navy. Later he served on the faculty of a major university and later transitioned to the electric utility business where he retired as a senior executive. In each role he developed leadership principles to improve the organization's performance. Since retiring, he has continued research in leadership and organization effectiveness applying this experience through consulting and writing.

Bryan S. Shriver, B.S.

> Bryan Shriver has enjoyed a career focused on applying technology to transform an organization's effectiveness and benefit to customers. He was among the early developers of a digital newspaper and later applied his technical and leadership skills to financial institutions. He currently serves as the Chief Technology Officer for a financial institution where he leads the digital transformation of personal and business finance.

Brandon B. Shriver, M.S., B.S.

> Brandon Shriver is the youngest member of the Three-Seven Research team. He has served as an engineer at an independent test facility and is now involved in the design of the next generation of industrial trucks. His degree in engineering management combined with a broad range of experience in the heavy truck industry provides a solid understanding of processes and oversight.

[i] NKJV designates Scripture taken from the New King James Version of the Bible ® Copyright © 1982 by Thomas Nelson. Used by permission. All rights reserved.

[ii] ESV designates Scripture taken from the ESV® Bible (The Holy Bible, English Standard Version®) copyright © 2001 by Crossway Bibles, a publishing ministry of Good News Publishers. Used by permission. All rights reserved.

www.ingramcontent.com/pod-product-compliance
Lightning Source LLC
Chambersburg PA
CBHW052211220526
45471CB00004B/1909